OBSERV  THE NATURE OF CIVIL LIBERTY

-THE PRINCIPLES OF GOVERNMENT, AND THE JUSTICE AND POLICY OF THE WAR WITH AMERICA-

Richard Price

Initially published in 1776

Table of Contents

PART I.

OUR Colonies in NORTH AMERICA appear to be now determined to risk and suffer every thing, under the persuasion, that GREAT BRITAIN is attempting to rob them of that Liberty to which every member of society, and all civil communities, have a natural and unalienable right. The question, therefore, whether this is a reasonable persuasion, is highly interesting, and deserves the most careful attention of every *Englishman* who values Liberty, and wishes to avoid staining himself with the guilt of invading it. But it is impossible to judge properly of this question without correct ideas of Liberty *in general;* and of the nature, limits, and principles of Civil Liberty *in particular.*—The following observations on this subject appear to me important, as well as just; and I cannot make myself easy without offering them to the Public at the present period, big with events of the last consequence to this kingdom. I do this, with reluctance and pain, urged by strong feelings, but at the same time checked by the consciousness that I am likely to deliver sentiments not favourable to the present measures of that government, under which I live, and to which I am a constant and zealous well-wisher. Such, however, are my present sentiments and views, that this is a consideration of inferior moment with me; and, as I hope never to go beyond the bounds of decent discussion and expostulation, I flatter myself, that I shall be able to avoid giving any person just cause of offence.

The observations with which I shall begin, are of a more general and abstracted nature; but being, in my opinion, of particular consequence; and necessary to introduce what I have principally in view, I hope they will be patiently read and considered.

SECT. I.: Of the Nature of Liberty in General.

IN order to obtain a more distinct and accurate view of the nature of Liberty as such, it will be useful to consider it under the four following general divisions.

First, *Physical* Liberty.—Secondly, *Moral* Liberty.—Thirdly, *Religious* Liberty.—And
Fourthly, *Civil* Liberty.—These heads comprehend under them all the different kinds of Liberty. And I have placed *Civil* Liberty last, because I mean to apply to it all I shall say of the other kinds of Liberty.

By PHYSICAL LIBERTY I mean that principle of *Spontaneity,* or *Self-determination,* which constitutes us *Agents;* or which gives us a command over our actions, rendering them properly *ours,* and not effects of the operation of any foreign cause.—MORAL LIBERTY is the power of following, in all circumstances, our sense of right and wrong; or of acting in conformity to our reflecting and moral principles, without being controuled by any contrary principles.—RELIGIOUS LIBERTY signifies the power of exercising, without molestation, that mode of religion which we think best; or of making the decisions of our own consciences, respecting religious truth, the rule of] our conduct, and not any of the decisions of others.—In like manner; CIVIL LIBERTY is the power of a *Civil Society* or *State* to govern itself by its own discretion; or by laws of its own making, without being subject to any foreign discretion, or to the impositions of any extraneous will or power.

It should be observed, that, according to these definitions of the different kinds of liberty, there is one general idea, that runs through them all; I mean, the idea of *Self-direction,* or *Self-government.*—Did our volitions originate not with *ourselves,* but with some cause over which we have no power; or were we under a necessity of always following some will different from our own, we should want PHYSICAL LIBERTY.

In like manner; he whose perceptions of moral obligation are controuled by his passions has lost his *Moral Liberty;* and the most common language applied to him is, that he wants *Self-government.*

He likewise who, in religion, cannot govern himself by his convictions of religious duty, but is obliged to receive formularies of faith, and to practise modes of worship imposed upon him by others, wants *Religious Liberty.*— And the Community also that is governed, not by itself, but by some will independent of it, and over which it has no controul, wants *Civil Liberty.*

In all these cases there is a force which stands opposed to the agent's *own* will; and which, as far as it operates, produces *Servitude.*—In the *first* case, this force is incompatible with the very idea of voluntary motion; and the subject of it is a mere passive instrument which never *acts,* but is always *acted upon.*—In the *second* case; this force is the influence of passion getting the better of reason; or the *brute*overpowering and conquering the will of the *man.*—In the *third* case; it is *Human Authority* in religion requiring conformity to particular modes of faith and worship, and superseding *private judgment.*—And in the last case, it is any will distinct from that of the Majority of a Community, which claims a power of making laws for it, and disposing of its property.

5

This it is, I think, that marks the limit, or that lays the line between *Liberty* and *Slavery*. As far as, in any instance, the operation of any cause comes in to restrain the power of Self-government, so far Slavery is introduced: Nor do I think that a preciser idea than this of Liberty and Slavery can be formed.

I cannot help wishing I could here fix my reader's attention, and engage him to consider carefully the dignity of that blessing to which we give the name of LIBERTY, according to the representation now made of it. There is not a word in the whole compass of language which expresses so much of what is important and excellent. It is, in every view of it, a blessing truly sacred and invaluable.—Without *Physical Liberty,* man would be a machine acted upon by mechanical springs, having no principle of motion in himself, or command over events; and, therefore, incapable of all merit and demerit.— Without *Moral Liberty* he is a wicked and detestable being, subject to the tyranny of base lusts, and the sport of every vile appetite.—And without *Religious* and *Civil Liberty* he is a poor and abject animal, without rights, without property, and without a conscience, bending his neck to the yoke, and crouching to the will of every silly creature who has the insolence to pretend to authority over him.— Nothing, therefore, can be of so much consequence to us as *Liberty*. It is the foundation of all honour, and the chief privilege and glory of our natures.

In fixing our ideas on the subject of Liberty, it is of particular use to take such an enlarged view of it as I have now given. But the immediate object of the present enquiry being *Civil Liberty,* I will confine to it all the subsequent observations.

]

SECT. II.: Of Civil Liberty and the Principles of Government.

FROM what has been said it is obvious, that all civil government, as far as it can be denominated *free,* is the creature of the people. It originates with them. It is conducted under their direction; and has in view nothing but their happiness. All its different forms are no more than so many different modes in which they chuse to direct their affairs, and to secure the quiet enjoyment of their rights.— In every free state every man is his own Legislator.— All *taxes* are free-gifts for public services.—All *laws* are particular provisions or regulations established by COMMON CONSENT for gaining protection and safety.—And all *Magistrates* are Trustees or Deputies for carrying these regulations into execution.

Liberty, therefore, is too imperfectly defined when it is said to be "a Government by LAWS, and not by MEN." If the laws are made by one man, or a junto of men in a state, and not by COMMON CONSENT, a government by them does not differ from Slavery. In this case it would be a contradiction in terms to say that the state governs itself.

From hence it is obvious that *Civil Liberty,* in its most perfect degree, can be enjoyed only in small states, where every member is capable of giving his suffrage in person, and of being chosen into public offices. When a state becomes so numerous, or when the different parts of it are removed to such distances from one another, as to render this impracticable, a diminution of Liberty necessarily arises. There are, however, in these circumstances, methods by which such near approaches may be made to perfect Liberty as shall answer all the purposes of government, and at the same time secure every right of human nature.

Tho' all the members of a state should not be capable of giving their suffrages on public
measures, *individually* and *personally,* they may do this by the appointment of *Substitutes* or *Representatives.* They may entrust the powers of legislation, subject to such restrictions as they shall think necessary, with any number of *Delegates;* and whatever can be done by such delegates within the limits of their trust, may be considered as done by the united voice and counsel of the Community.—In this method a free government may be established in the largest state; and it is conceivable that by regulations of this kind, any number of states might be subjected to a scheme of government, that would exclude the desolations of war, and produce universal peace and order.

Let us think here of what may be practicable in this way with respect to *Europe* in particular.—While it continues divided, as it is at present, into a great number of independent kingdoms whose interests are continually clashing, it is impossible but that disputes will often arise which must end in war and carnage. It would be no remedy to this evil to make one of these states supreme over the rest; and to give it an absolute plenitude of power to superintend and controul them. This would be to subject all the states to the arbitrary discretion of one, and to establish an ignominious slavery not possible to be long endured. It would, therefore, be a remedy worse than the disease; nor is it possible it should be approved by any mind that has not lost every idea of Civil Liberty. On the contrary.—Let every state, with respect to all its internal concerns, be continued independent of all the rest; and let a general confederacy be formed by the appointment of a SENATE consisting of Representatives from all the different states. Let this SENATE possess the power of managing all the *common* concerns of the united states, and of judging and deciding between them, as a common *Arbiter* or *Umpire,* in all disputes; having, at the same time, under its direction, the common force of the states to support its decisions.—In these circumstances, each separate state would be secure against the interference of foreign power in its private concerns, and, therefore, would possess *Liberty;* and at] the same time it would be secure against all oppression and insult from every neighbouring state.—Thus might the scattered force and abilities of a whole continent be gathered into one point; all litigations settled as they rose; universal peace preserved; and nation prevented *from any more lifting up a sword against nation.*

I have observed, that tho', in a great state, all the individuals that compose it cannot be admitted to an immediate participation in the powers of legislation and government, yet they may participate in these powers by a delegation of them to a body of representatives.—In this case it is evident that the state will be still *free* or *self-governed;* and that it will be more or less so in proportion as it is more or less fairly and adequately represented. If the persons to whom the trust of government is committed hold their places for short terms; if they are chosen by the unbiassed voices of a majority of the state, and subject to their instructions: Liberty will be enjoyed in its highest degree. But if they are chosen for long terms by a part only of the state; and if during that term they are subject to no controul from their constituents; the very idea of Liberty will be lost, and the power of chusing representatives becomes nothing but a power, lodged in a *few,* to chuse at certain periods, a body of *Masters* for themselves and for the rest of the Community. And if a state is so sunk that the majority of its representatives are elected by a handful of the meanest (*a*)persons in it, whose votes are always paid for; and if also, there is a higher will on which even these mock representatives themselves depend, and that directs their voices: In these circumstances, it will be an abuse of language to say that the state possesses Liberty. Private men, indeed, might be allowed the exercise of Liberty; as they might also under the most despotic government; but it would be an *indulgence* or *connivance* derived from the spirit of the times, or from an accidental mildness in the administration. And, rather than be governed in such a manner, it would perhaps be better to be governed by the will of one man without any representation: For a representation so degenerated could answer no other end than to mislead and deceive, by disguising slavery, and keeping up a *form* of Liberty when the *reality* was lost.

Within the limits now mentioned, Liberty may be enjoyed in every possible degree; from that which is complete and perfect, to that which is merely nominal; according as the people have more or less of a share in government, and of a controuling power over the persons by whom it is administered.

In general, to be *free* is to be guided by one's own will; and to be guided by the will of another is the characteristic of *Servitude.* This is particularly applieable to Political Liberty. That state, I have observed, is *free,* which is guided by its own will; or, (which comes to the same) by the will of an assembly of representatives appointed by itself and accountable to itself. And every state that is not so governed; or in which a body of men representing the people make not an essential part of the Legislature, is in *slavery.*—In order to form the most perfect constitution of government, there may be the best reasons for joining to such a body of representatives, an *Hereditary Council,* consisting of men of the first rank in the state, with a *Supreme executive Magistrate* at the head of all. This will form useful checks in a legislature; and contribute to give it vigour, union, and dispatch, without infringing liberty: for, as long as that part of a government which represents the people is a *fair representation;* and also has a negative on all public measures, together with the sole power of] imposing taxes and originating supplies; the essentials of Liberty will be preserved.—We make it our boast in this country, that this is our own constitution. I will not say with how much reason.

Of such Liberty as I have now described, it is impossible that there should be an excess. Government is an institution for the benefit of the people governed, which they have power to model as they please; and to say, that they can have too much of this power, is to say, that there ought to be a power in the state superior to that which gives it being, and from which all jurisdiction in it is derived.— Licentiousness, which has been commonly mentioned, as an extreme of liberty, is indeed its opposite. It is government by the will of rapacious individuals, in opposition to the will of the community, made known and declared in the laws. A free state, at the same time that it is free itself, makes all its members free by excluding licentiousness, and guarding their persons and property and good name against insult. It is the end of all just government, at the same time that it secures the liberty of the public against *foreign* injury, to secure the liberty of the individual against *private* injury. I do not, therefore, think it strictly just to say, that it belongs to the nature of government to entrench on private liberty. It ought never to do this, except as far as the exercise of private liberty encroaches on the liberties of others. That is; it is licentiousness it restrains, and liberty itself only when used to destroy liberty.

It appears from hence, that licentiousness and despotism are more nearly allied than is commonly imagined. They are both alike inconsistent with liberty, and the true end of government; nor is there any other difference between them, than that the one is the licentiousness of *great* men, and the other the licentiousness of *little* men; or that, by the one, the persons and property of a people are subject to outrage and invasion from a King, or a lawless body of *Grandees;* and that, by the other, they are subject to the like outrage from a *lawless mob*—In avoiding one of these evils, mankind have often run into the other. But all well-constituted governments guard equally against both. Indeed of the two, the last is, on several accounts, the least to be dreaded, and has done the least mischief. It may be truly said, that if licentiousness has destroyed its thousands, despotism has destroyed its millions. The former, having little power, and no system to support it, necessarily finds its own remedy; and a people soon get out of the tumult and anarchy attending it. But a despotism, wearing the form of government, and being armed with its force, is an evil not to be conquered without dreadful struggles. It goes on from age to age, debasing the human faculties, levelling all distinctions, and preying on the rights and blessings of society.—It deserves to be added, that in a state disturbed by licentiousness, there is an animation which is favourable to the human mind, and which puts it upon exerting its powers. But in a state habituated to a despotism; all is still and torpid. A dark and savage tyranny stifles every effort of genius; and the mind loses all its spirit and dignity.

Before I proceed to what I have farther in view, I will observe, that the account now given of the principles of public Liberty, and the nature of an equal and free government, shews what judgment we should form of that OMNIPOTENCE, which, it has been said, must belong to every government as such. Great stress has been laid on this, but most unreasonably.—Government, as has been before observed, is, in the very nature of it, a TRUST; and all its powers a DELEGATION for gaining particular ends.

This *trust* may be misapplied and abused. It may be employed to deseat the very ends for which it was instituted; and to subvert the very rights which it ought to protect.—A PARLIAMENT, for instance, consisting of a body of representatives, chosen for a limited period, to make laws, and to grant money for public services, would forfeit its authority by making itself porpetual, or even prolonging its] own duration; by nominating its own members; by accepting bribes; or subjecting itself to any kind of foreign influence. This would convert a *Parliament* into a *conclave* or *junto* of self-created tools; and a state that has lost its regard to its own rights, so far as to submit to such a breach of trust in its rulers, is enslaved.—Nothing, therefore, can be more absurd than the doctrine which some have taught, with respect to the omnipotence of parliaments. They possess no power beyond the limits of the trust for the execution of which they were formed. If they contradict this trust, they betray their constituents, and dissolve themselves. All delegated power must be subordinate and limited.—If omnipotence can, with any sense, be ascribed to a legislature, it must be lodged where all legislative authority originates; that is, in the PEOPLE. For *their* sakes government is instituted; and their's is the only real omnipotence.

I am sensible, that all I have been saying would be very absurd, were the opinions just which some have maintained concerning the origin of government. According to these opinions, government is not the creature of the people, or the result of a convention between them and their rulers: But there are certain men who possess in themselves, independently of the will of the people, a right of governing them, which they derive from the Deity. This doctrine has been abundantly refuted by many(a) excellent writers. It is a doctrine which avowedly subverts Civil Liberty; and which represents mankind as a body of vassals, formed to descend like cattle from one set of owners to another, who have an absolute dominion over them. It is a wonder, that those who view their species in a light so humiliating, should ever be able to think of themselves without regret and shame. The intention of these observations is not to oppose such sentiments; but, taking for granted the reasonableness of Civil Liberty, to shew wherein it consists, and what distinguishes it from its contrary.—And, in considering this subject, as it has been now treated, it is unavoidable to reflect on the excellency of a free government, and its tendency to exalt the nature of man.—Every member of a free state, having his property secure, and knowing himself his own governor, possesses a consciousness of dignity in himself, and feels incitements to emulation and improvement, to which the miserable slaves of arbitrary power must be utter strangers. In such a state all the springs of action have room to operate, and the mind is stimulated to the noblest exertions(b).—But to be obliged, from our birth, to look up to a creature no better than ourselves as the master of our fortunes; and to receive his will as our law— What can be more humiliating? What elevated ideas can enter a mind in such a situation?—Agreeably to this remark; the subjects of free states have, in all ages, been most distinguished for genius and knowledge. Liberty is the soil where the arts and sciences have flourished; and the more free a state has been, the more have the powers of the human mind been drawn forth into action, and the greater number of brave men has it produced. With what lustre do the antient free states of *Greece* shine in the annals of the world? How different is that country now, under the Great *Turk?* The difference between a country inhabited by men, and by brutes, is not greater.

These are reflexions which should be constantly present to every mind in this country.—As *Moral* Liberty is the prime blessing of man in his *private* capacity, so is *Civil* Liberty in his *public* capacity. There is nothing that requires more to be *watched* than power. There is nothing that ought to be opposed with a more determined resolution than its encroachments. Sleep in a state, as *Montesquieu* says, is always followed by slavery.

]

The people of this kingdom were once warmed by such sentiments as these. Many a sycophant of power have they sacrificed. Often have they fought and bled in the cause of Liberty. But that time seems to be going. The fair inheritance of Liberty left us by our ancestors many of us are not unwilling to resign. An abandoned venality, the inseparable companion of dissipation and extravagance, has poisoned the springs of public virtue among us: And should any events ever arise that should render the same opposition necessary that took place in the times of King *Charles* the First, and *James* the Second, I am afraid all that is valuable to us would be lost. The terror of the standing army, the danger of the public funds, and the all-corrupting influence of the treasury, would deaden all zeal, and produce general acquiescence and servility.

SECT. III.: Of the Authority of one Country over another.

FROM the nature and principles of Civil Liberty, as they have been now explained, it is an immediate and necessary inference, that no one community can have any power over the property or legislation of another community, that is not incorporated with it by a just and adequate representation.—Then only, it has been shewn, is a state *free,* when it is governed by its own will. But a country that is subject to the legislature of another country, in which it has no voice, and over which it has no controul, cannot be said to be governed by its own will. Such a country, therefore, is in a state of slavery. And it deserves to be particularly considered, that such a slavery is worse, on several accounts, than any slavery of private men to one another, or of kingdoms to despots within themselves.— Between one state and another, there is none of that fellow-feeling that takes place between persons in private life. Being detached bodies that never see one another, and residing perhaps in different quarters of the globe, the state that governs cannot be a witness to the sufferings occasioned by its oppressions; or a competent judge of the circumstances and abilities of the people who are governed. They must also have in a great degree separate interests; and the more the one is loaded, the more the other may be eased. The infamy likewise of oppression, being in such circumstances shared among a multitude, is not likely to be much felt or regarded.—On all these accounts there is, in the case of one country subjugated to another, little or nothing to check rapacity; and the most flagrant injustice and cruelty may be practised without remorse or pity.—I will add, that it is particularly difficult to shake off a tyranny of this kind. A single despot, if a people are unanimous and resolute, may be soon subdued. But a despotic state is not easily subdued; and a people subject to it cannot emancipate themselves without entering into a dreadful, and, perhaps, very unequal contest.

I cannot help observing farther, that the slavery of a people to internal despots may be qualified and limited; but I don't see what can limit the authority of one state over another. The exercise of power in this case can have no other measure than discretion; and, therefore, must be indefinite and absolute.

Once more. It should be considered that the government of one country by another, can only be supported by a military force; and, without such a support, must be destitute of all weight and efficiency.

This will be best explained by putting the following case.— There is, let us suppose, in a province subject to the sovereignty of a distant state, a subordinate legislature consisting of an Assembly chosen by the people; a Council chosen by that Assembly; and a Governor *appointed* by the Sovereign State, and paid by the Province. There are likewise, judges and other officers, appointed and paid in the same manner, for administering *justice* agreeably to the laws, by the verdicts of juries fairly and indiscriminately chosen.—This forms a constitution seemingly free, by giving the people a share in their own government,] and some check on their rulers. But, while there is a higher legislative power, to the controul of which such a constitution is subject, it does not itself possess Liberty, and therefore, cannot be of any use as a security to Liberty; nor is it possible that it should be of long duration. Laws offensive to the Province will be enacted by the Sovereign State. The legislature of the Province will remonstrate against them. The magistrates will not execute them. Juries will not convict upon them; and consequently, like the Pope's Bulls which once governed *Europe,* they will become nothing but forms and empty sounds, to which no regard will be shewn.—In order to remedy this evil, and to give efficiency to its government, the supreme state will naturally be led to withdraw the *Governor,* the *Council,* and the *Judges(a)* from the controul of the Province, by making them entirely dependent on itself for
their *pay* and *continuance in office,* as well as for their appointment. It will also alter the mode of chusing Juries on purpose to bring them more under its influence: And in some cases, under the pretence of the impossibility of

gaining an impartial trial where government is resisted, it will perhaps ordain, that offenders shall be removed from the Province to be tried within its own territories: And it may even go so far in this kind of policy, as to endeavour to prevent the effects of discontents, by forbidding all meetings and associations of the people, except at such times, and for such particular purposes, as shall be permitted them.

Thus will such a Province be exactly in the same state that *Britain* would be in, were our first executive magistrate, our House of Lords, and our Judges, nothing but the instruments of a foreign democratical power; were our Juries nominated by that power; or were we liable to be transported to a distant country to be tried for offences committed here; and restrained from calling any meetings, consulting about any grievances, or associating for any purposes, except when leave should be given us by a *Lord Lieutenant* or *Viceroy.*

It is certain that this is a state of oppression which no country could endure, and to which it would be vain to expect, that any people should submit an hour without an armed force to compel them.

The late transactions in *Massachusett*'s *Bay* are a perfect exemplification of what I have now said. The government of *Great Britain* in that Province has gone on exactly in the train I have described; till at last it became necessary to station troops there, not amenable to the civil power; and all terminated in a government by the SWORD. And such, if a people are not sunk below the character of men, will be the issue of all government in similar circumstances.

It may be asked—"Are there not causes by which one state may acquire a *rightful* authority over another, though not consolidated by an adequate Representation?"—I]answer, that there are no such causes.—All the causes to which such an effect *can* be ascribed are CONQUEST, COMPACT,or OBLIGATIONS CONFERRED.

Much has been said of the right of *conquest;* and history contains little more than accounts of kingdoms reduced by it under the dominion of other kingdoms, and of the havock it has made among mankind. But the authority derived from hence, being founded on violence, is never *rightful.* The *Roman Republic* was nothing but a faction against the general liberties of the world; and had no more right to give law to the Provinces subject to it, than thieves have to the property they seize, or to the houses into which they break.—Even in the case of a just war undertaken by one people to defend itself against the oppressions of another people, conquest gives only a right to an indemnification for the injury which occasioned the war, and a reasonable security against future injury.

Neither can any state require such an authority over other states in virtue of any *compacts* or *cessions.* This is a case in which compacts are not binding. *Civil* Liberty is, in this respect, on the same footing with *Religious* Liberty. As no people can lawfully surrender their *Religious* Liberty, by giving up their right of judging for themselves in religion, or by allowing any human beings to prescribe to them what faith they shall embrace, or what mode of worship they shall practise; so neither can any civil societies lawfully surrender their *Civil* Liberty, by giving up to any extraneous jurisdiction their power of legislating for themselves and disposing their property. Such a cession, being inconsistent with the unalienable rights of human nature, would either not bind at all; or bind only the individuals who made it. This is a blessing which no one generation of men can give up for another; and which, when lost, a people have always a right to resume.—Had our ancestors in this country been so mad as to have subjected themselves to any foreign Community, we could not have been under any obligation to continue in such a state. And all the nations now in the world who, in consequence of the tameness and folly of their predecessors, are subject to arbitrary power, have a right to emancipate themselves as soon as they can.

If neither *conquest* nor *compact* can give such an authority, much less can any favours received, or any services performed by one state for another.—Let the favour received be what it will, Liberty is too dear a price for it. A state that has been *obliged* is not, therefore, bound to be *enslaved*. It ought, if possible, to make an adequate return for the services done to it; but to suppose that it ought to give up the power of governing itself, and the disposal of its property, would be to suppose, that, in order to shew its gratitude, it ought to part with the power of ever afterwards exercising gratitude.—How much has been done by this kingdom for *Hanover?* But no one will say that on this account, we have a right to make the laws of *Hanover;* or even to draw a single penny from it without its own consent.

After what has been said it will, I am afraid, be trifling to apply the preceding arguments to the case of different communities, which are considered as different parts of the same *Empire*. But there are reasons which render it necessary for me to be explicit in making this application.

What I mean here is just to point out the difference of situation between communities forming an *Empire;* and particular bodies or classes of men forming different parts of a *Kingdom*. Different communities forming an *Empire* have no connexions, which produce a necessary reciprocation of interests between them. They inhabit different districts, and are governed by different legislatures.—On the contrary. The different classes of men *within* a *kingdom* are all placed on the same ground. Their concerns and interests are the same; and what is done to one part must affect all.—These are situations totally different; and a] constitution of government that may be consistent with Liberty in one of them, may be entirely inconsistent with it in the other. It is, however, certain that, even in the last of these situations, no one part ought to govern the rest. In order to a fair and equal government, there ought to be a fair and equal representation of all that are governed; and as far as this is wanting in any government, it deviates from the principles of Liberty, and becomes unjust and oppressive.—But in the circumstances of different communities, all this holds with unspeakably more force. The government of a part in this case becomes complete tyranny; and subjection to it becomes complete slavery.

But ought there not, it is asked, to exist somewhere in an *Empire* a supreme legislative authority over the whole; or a power to controul and bind all the different states of which it consists?—This enquiry has been already answered. The truth is, that such a supreme controuling power ought to exist no-where except in such a SENATE or body of delegates as that described in page 7; and that the authority or supremacy of even this senate ought to be limited to the common concerns of the *Empire*.—I think I have proved that the fundamental principles of Liberty necessarily require this.

In a word. An *Empire* is a collection of states or communities united by some common bond or tye. If these states have each of them free constitutions of government, and, with respect to taxation and internal legislation, are independent of the other states, but united by compacts, or alliances, or subjection to a Great *Council,* representing the whole, or to one monarch entrusted with the supreme executive power: In these circumstances, the Empire will be an Empire of Freemen.—If, on the contrary, like the different provinces subject to the *Grand Seignior,* none of the states possess any independent legislative authority; but are all subject to an absolute monarch, whose will is their law, then is the Empire an Empire of Slaves.—If one of the states is free, but governs by its will all the other states; then is the Empire, like that of the Romans in the times of the republic, an Empire consisting of one state free, and the rest in slavery: Nor does it make any more difference in this case, that the governing state is itself free, than it does in the case of a kingdom subject to a *despot,* that this despot is himself free. I have before observed, that this only makes the slavery worse. There is, in the one case, a chance, that in the quick succession of despots, a good one will sometimes arise. But bodies of men continue the same; and have generally proved the most unrelenting of all tyrants.

A great writer before(a) quoted, observes of the *Roman Empire,* that while Liberty was at the center, tyranny prevailed in the distant provinces; that such as were free under it were extremely so, while those who were slaves groaned under the extremity of slavery; and that the same events that *destroyed* the liberty of the former, *gave* liberty to the latter.

The Liberty of the *Romans,* therefore, was only an additional calamity to the provinces governed by them; and though it might have been said of the *citizens* of *Rome,* that they were the "freest members of any civil society in the known world;" yet of the *subjects* of *Rome,* it must have been said, that they were the completest slaves in the

22

known world.—How remarkable is it, that this very people, once the freest of mankind, but at the same time the most proud and tyrannical, should become at last the most contemptible and abject slaves that ever existed?

]

PART II.

IN the foregoing disquisitions, I have, from one leading principle, deduced a number of consequences, that seems to me incapable of being disputed. I have meant that they should be applied to the great question between this kingdom and the Colonies which has occasioned the present war with them.

It is impossible but my readers must have been all along making this application; and if they still think that the claims of this kingdom are reconcilable to the principles of true liberty and legitimate government, I am afraid, that nothing I shall farther say will have any effect on their judgments. I wish, however, they would have the patience and candour to go with me, and grant me a hearing some time longer.

Though clearly decided in my own judgment on this subject, I am inclined to make great allowances for the different judgments of others. We have been so used to speak of the Colonies as *our* Colonies, and to think of them as in a state of subordination to us, and as holding their existence in *America* only for our use, that it is no wonder the prejudices of many are alarmed, when they find a different doctrine maintained. The meanest person among us is disposed to look upon himself as having a body of subjects in *America;* and to be offended at the denial of his right to make laws for them, though perhaps he does not

know what colour they are of, or what language they talk—
Such are the natural prejudices of this country.—But the
time is coming, I hope, when the unreasonableness of them
will be seen; and more just sentiments prevail.

Before I proceed, I beg it may be attended to, that I have
chosen to try this question by the general principles of Civil
Liberty; and not by the practice of former times; or by
the *Charters* granted the colonies.—The
arguments *for* them, drawn from these last topics, appear to
me greatly to outweigh the arguments *against* them. But I
wish to have this question brought to a higher test, and
surer issue. The question with all liberal enquirers ought to
be, not what jurisdiction over them *Precedents,*
Statutes, and *Charters* give, but what reason and equity, and
the rights of humanity give.—This is, in truth, a question
which no kingdom has ever before had occasion to agitate.
The case of a free country branching itself out in the
manner *Britain* has done, and sending to a distant world
colonies which have there, from small beginnings, and
under free legislatures of their own, increased, and formed
a body of powerful states, likely soon to become superior to
the parent state—This is a case which is new in the history
of mankind; and it is extremely improper to judge of it by
the rules of any narrow and partial policy; or to consider it
on any other ground than the general one of reason and
justice.—Those who will be candid enough to judge on this
ground, and who can divest themselves of national
prejudices, will not, I fancy, remain long unsatisfied.—But
alas! Matters are gone too far. The dispute probably must
be settled another way; and the sword alone, I am afraid, is
now to determine what the rights
of *Britain* and *America* are.—Shocking situation!—
Detested be the measures which have brought us into it:
And, if we are endeavouring to enforce injustice, cursed
will be the war.—A retreat, however, is not yet

impracticable. The duty we owe our gracious sovereign obliges us to rely on his disposition to stay the sword, and to promote the happiness of all the different parts of the Empire at the head of which he is placed. With some hopes, therefore, that it may not be too late to reason on this subject, I will, in the following Sections, enquire what the war with *America* is in the following respects.

]

- 1. In respect of Justice.
- 2. The Principles of the Constitution.
- 3. In respect of Policy and Humanity.
- 4. The Honour of the Kingdom.

And lastly, The Probability of succeeding in it.

SECT. I.: Of the Justice of the War with America.

THE enquiry, whether the war with the Colonies is a *just*war, will be best determined by stating the power over them, which it is the end of the war to maintain: And this cannot be better done, than in the words of an act of parliament, made on purpose to define it. That act, it is well known, declares, "That this kingdom has power, and of right ought to have power to make laws and statutes to bind the Colonies, and people of *America,* in all cases whatever."—Dreadful power indeed! I defy any one to express slavery in stronger language. It is the same with declaring "that we have a right to do with them what we please."—I will not waste my time by applying to such a claim any of the preceding arguments. If my reader does not feel more in this case, than words can express, all reasoning must be vain.

25

But, probably, most persons will be for using milder language; and for saying no more than, that the united legislatures of *England* and *Scotland* have of right power to tax the Colonies, and a supremacy of legislation over *America.*—But this comes to the same. If it means any thing, it means, that the property, and the legislations of the Colonies, are subject to the absolute discretion of *Great Britain,* and ought of right to be so. The nature of the thing admits of no limitation. The Colonies can never be admitted to be judges, how far the authority over them in these cases shall extend. This would be to destroy it entirely.—If *any*part of their property is subject to our discretion, the whole must be so. If we have a right to interfere at all in their internal legislations, we have a right to interfere as far as we think proper.—It is self-evident, that this leaves them nothing they can call *their own.*—And what is it that can give to any people such a supremacy over another people?—I have already examined the principal answers which have been given to this enquiry. But it will not be amiss in this place to go over some of them again.

It has been urged, that such a right must be lodged somewhere, "in order to preserve the UNITY of the British Empire."

Pleas of this sort have, in all ages, been used to justify tyranny.—They have in RELIGION given rise to numberless oppressive claims, and slavish Hierarchies. And in the *Romish Communion* particularly, it is well known, that the POPE claims the title and powers of the supreme head on earth of the Christian church, in order to preserve its UNITY.—With respect to the *British Empire,* nothing can be more preposterous than to endeavour to maintain its unity, by setting up such a claim. This is a method of establishing unity, which, like the similar method in

religion, can produce nothing but discord and mischief.—
The truth is, that a common relation to one supreme
executive head; an exchange of kind offices; tyes of interest
and affection, and *compacts,* are sufficient to give the
British Empire all the unity that is necessary. But if not—If,
in order to preserve its *Unity,* one half of it must be
enslaved to the other half, let it, in the name of God, want
Unity.

Much has been said of "the *Superiority* of the British
State." But what gives us our superiority?—Is it
our *Wealth?*—This never confers real dignity. On the
contrary: Its effect is always to debase, intoxicate, and
corrupt.—Is it the *number of our people?* The colonies will
soon be equal to us in number.—Is it
our *Knowledge* and *Virtue?* They are
probably *equally* knowing,] and *more* virtuous There are
names among them that will not stoop to any names among
the philosophers and politicians of this island.

"But we are the PARENT STATE."—These are the magic
words which have fascinated and misled us.—The English
came from *Germany.* Does that give the *German* states a
right to tax us?—Children, having no property, and being
incapable of guiding themselves, the Author of nature has
committed the care of them to their parents, and subjected
them to their absolute authority. But there is a period when,
having acquired property, and a capacity of judging for
themselves, they become independent agents; and when,
for this reason, the authority of their parents ceases, and
becomes nothing but the respect and influence due to
benefactors. Supposing, therefore, that the order of nature
in establishing the relation between parents and children,
ought to have been the rule of our conduct to the Colonies,
we should have been gradually relaxing our authority as
they grew up. But, like mad parents, we have done the

contrary; and, at the very time when our authority should have been most relaxed, we have carried it to the greatest extent, and exercised it with the greatest rigour. No wonder then, that they have turned upon us; and obliged us to remember, that they are not Children.

"But we have," it is said, "protected them, and run deeply in debt on their "account."—The full answer to this has been already given, (page 13.) Will any one say, that all we have done for them has not been more on our *own* account,(*a*)than on *theirs?*—But suppose the contrary. Have they done nothing for us? Have they made no compensation for the protection they have received? Have they not helped us to pay our *taxes,* to support our poor, and to bear the burthen of our debts, by taking from us, at our own price, all the commodities with which we can supply them?—Have they not, for our advantage, submitted to many restraints in acquiring property? Must they likewise resign to us the disposal of that property?— Has not their exclusive trade with us been for many years one of the chief sources of our national wealth and power?—In all our wars have they not sought by our side, and contributed much to our success? In the last war, particularly, it is well known, that they ran themselves deeply in debt; and that the parliament thought it necessary to grant them considerable sums annually as compensations for going beyond their abilities in assisting us. And in this course would they have continued for many future years; perhaps, for ever.—In short; were an accurate account stated, it is by no means certain which side would appear to be most indebted. When asked as *freemen,* they have hitherto seldom discovered any reluctance in giving. But, in obedience to a demand, and with the bayonet at their breasts, they will give us nothing but blood.

It is farther said, "that the land on which they settled was ours."—But how same it to be ours? If sailing along a coast can give a right to a country, then might the people of *Japan* become, as soon as they please, the proprietors of *Britain.* Nothing can be more chimerical than property founded on such a reason. If the land on which the Colonies first settled had any proprietors, they were the natives. The greatest part of it they bought of the natives. They] have since cleared and cultivated it; and, without any help from us, converted a wilderness into fruitful and pleasant fields. It is, therefore, now on a double account their property; and no power on earth can have any right to disturb them in the possession of it, or to take from them, without their consent, any part of its produce.

But let it be granted that the land was ours. Did they not settle upon it under the faith of charters, which promised them the enjoyment of all the rights of *Englishmen,* and allowed them to tax themselves, and to be governed by legislatures of their own, similar to ours? These charters were given them by an authority, which at the time was thought competent; and they have been rendered sacred by an acquiescence on our part for more than a century. Can it then be wondered at, that the Colonies should revolt, when they found their charters violated; and an attempt made to force INNOVATIONS upon them by famine and the sword?— But I lay no stress on charters. They derive their rights from a higher source. It is inconsistent with common sense to imagine, that any people would ever think of settling in a distant country, on any such condition, as that the people from whom they withdrew, should for ever be masters of their property, and have power to subject them to any modes of government they pleased. And had there been express stipulations to this purpose in all the charters of the colonies, they would, in my opinion, be no more bound by them, than if it had been stipulated with them, that they should go naked, or expose themselves to the incursions of wolves and tigers.

The defective state of the representation of this kingdom has been farther pleaded to prove our right to tax *America*. *We*submit to a parliament that does not represent us, and therefore *they* ought.—How strange an argument is this? It is saying we want liberty; and therefore, they ought to want it.—Suppose it true, that they are indeed contending for a better constitution of government, and more liberty than we enjoy: Ought this to make us angry?—Who is there that does not see the danger to which this country is exposed?— Is it generous, because we are in a sink, to endeavour to draw them into it? Ought we not rather to wish earnestly, that there may at least be ONE FREE COUNTRY left upon earth, to which we may fly, when venality, luxury, and vice have completed the ruin of Liberty here?

It is, however, by no means true, that *America* has no more right to be exempted from taxation by the *British*parliament, than *Britain* itself.—*Here,* all freeholders, and burgesses in boroughs, are represented. *There,* not one *Freeholder,* or any other person, is represented.—*Here,* the *aids* granted by the represented part of the kingdom must be proportionably *paid* by themselves; and the laws they make for *others,* they at the same time make for *themselves.* *There,* the aids they would grant would not be *paid,* but *received,* by themselves; and the laws they made would be made for *others only.*—In short. The relation of one country to another country, whose representatives have the power of taxing it (and of appropriating the money raised by the taxes) is much the same with the relation of a country to a single despot, or a body of despots, within itself, invested with the like power. In both cases, the people taxed and those who tax have separate interests; nor can there be any thing to check oppression, besides either the abilities of the people taxed, or the humanity of the *taxers*.—But indeed I can never hope to convince that person of any thing, who does not see an essential difference(a) between the two cases now mentioned; or between the circumstances of individuals, and classes of men, making parts of a community imperfectly represented in the legislature]that governs it; and the circumstances of a whole community, in a distant world, not at all represented.

But enough has been said by others on this point; nor is it possible for me to throw any new light upon it. To finish, therefore, what I meant to offer under this head, I must beg that the following considerations may be particularly attended to.

The question now between us and the Colonies is, Whether, in respect of taxation and internal legislation, they are bound to be subject to the jurisdiction of this kingdom: Or, in other words, Whether the *British* parliament has or has not of right a power to dispose of their property, and to model as it pleases their governments?—To this supremacy over them, we say, we are entitled; and in order to maintain it, we have begun the present war.—Let me here enquire,

1*st*. Whether, if we have now this supremacy, we shall not be equally entitled to it in any future time?—They are now but little short of half our number. To this number they have grown, from a small body of original settlers, by a very rapid increase. The probability is, that they will go on to increase; and that, in 50 or 60 years, they will be *double* our number;(a) and form a mighty Empire, consisting of a variety of states, all equal or superior to ourselves in all the arts and accomplishments, which give dignity and happiness to human life. In that period, will they be still bound to acknowledge that supremacy over them which we now claim? Can there be any person who will assert this; or whose mind does not revolt at the idea of a vast continent, holding all that is valuable to it, at the discretion of a handful of people on the other side the *Atlantic?*—But if, at that period, this would be unreasonable; what makes it otherwise *now?*—Draw the line, if you can.—But there is a still greater difficulty.

Britain is now, I will suppose, the seat of Liberty and Virtue; and its legislature consists of a body of able and independent men, who govern with wisdom and justice. The time may come when all will be reversed: When its excellent constitution of Government will be subverted: When, pressed by debts and taxes, it will be greedy to draw to itself an increase of revenue from every distant Province, in order to ease its own burdens: When the influence of the crown, strengthened by luxury and an universal profligacy of manners, will have tainted every heart, broken down every fence of Liberty, and rendered us a nation of tame and contented vassals: When a General *Election* will be nothing but a General *Auction* of *Boroughs:* And when the PARLIAMENT, the Grand Council of the nation, and once the faithful guardian of the state, and a terror to evil ministers, will be degenerated into a body of *Sycophants,* dependent and venal, always ready to confirm *any* measures; and little more than a public court for registering royal edicts.—Such, it is possible, may, some time or other, be the state of *Great Britain.*—What will, at that period, be the duty of the Colonies? Will they be still bound to unconditional submission? Must they always continue an appendage to our government; and follow it implicitly through every change that can happen to it?—Wretched condition, indeed, of millions of freemen as good as ourselves!—Will you say that we now govern equitably; and that there is no danger of any such revolution?—Would to God this were true!—But will you not always say the same? Who shall judge whether we govern equitably or not? Can you give the Colonies any *security* that such a period will never come? Once more.

If we have indeed that power which we claim over the legislations, and internal rights of the Colonies, may we not, whenever we please, subject them] to the arbitrary power of the crown?—I do not mean, that this would be a disadvantageous change: For I have before observed, that if a people are to be subject to an external power over which they have no command, it is better that power should be lodged in the hands of one man than of a multitude. But many persons think otherwise; and such ought to consider that, if this would be a calamity, the condition of the Colonies must be deplorable "A government by King, Lords, and Commons, (it has been said) is the perfection of government;" and so it is, when the Commons are a just representation of the people; and when also, it is not extended to any distant people, or communities, not represented. But if this is the *best,* a government by a king only must be the *worst;* and every claim implying a right to establish such a government among any people must be unjust and cruel.—It is self-evident, that by claiming a right to alter the constitutions of the Colonies, according to our discretion, we claim this power: And it is a power that we have thought fit to exercise in *one* of our Colonies; and that we have attempted to exercise in *another.*—
Canada, according to the late extension of its limits, is a country almost as large as half *Europe;* and it may possibly come in time to be filled with *British* subjects.
The *Quebec* act makes the king of *Great Britain* a despot over all that country.—In the Province
of *Massachusett's Bay* the same thing has been attempted and begun.

The act for BETTER *regulating their government,* passed at the same time with the *Quebec* act, gives the king the right of appointing, and removing at his pleasure, the members of one part of the legislature; alters the mode of chusing juries, on purpose to bring it more under the influence of the king; and takes away from the province the power of calling any meetings of the people without the king's consent.*(a)*—The judges, likewise, have been made dependent on the king, for their nomination and pay, and continuance in office.—If all this is no more than we have a right to do; may we not go on to abolish the house of representatives, to destroy all trials by juries, and to give up the province absolutely and totally to the will of the king?—May we not even establish popery in the province, as has been lately done in *Canada,* leaving the support of protestantism to the king's discretion?—Can there be any Englishman who, were it his own case, would not sooner lose his heart's blood than yield to claims so pregnant with evils, and destructive to every thing that can distinguish a *Freeman* from a *Slave?*

I will take this opportunity to add, that what I have now said, suggests a consideration that demonstrates, on how different a footing the Colonies are with respect to our government, from particular bodies of men *within* the kingdom, who happen not to be represented. Here, it is impossible that the represented part should subject the unrepresented part to arbitrary power, without including themselves. But in the Colonies it is *not* impossible. We know that it *has* been done.

SECT. II.: *Whether the War with* America *is justified by the Principles of the Constitution.*

I Have proposed, in the next place, to examine the war with the Colonies by the principles of the constitution.—I know, that it is common to say that we are now maintaining the constitution in *America*. If this means that we are endeavouring to establish our own constitution of government there; it is by no means true; nor, were it true, would it be right. They have chartered governments of their own, with which they are pleased; and which, if any power on earth may change without their consent, that power may likewise, if it thinks proper, deliver them over to the *Grand Seignior.*—Suppose the Colonies of *France* and *Spain* had, by compacts, enjoyed for near a century and a half, free]governments open to all the world, and under which they had grown and flourished; what should we think of those kingdoms, were they to attempt to destroy their governments, and to force upon them their own mode of government? Should we not applaud any zeal they discovered in repelling such an injury?—But the truth is, in the present instance, that we are not maintaining but violating our own constitution in *America*. The essence of our constitution consists in its independency. There is in this case no difference
between *subjection* and *annihilation*. Did, therefore, the Colonies possess governments perfectly the same with ours, the attempt to subject them to ours would be an attempt to ruin them. A free government loses its nature from the moment it becomes liable to be commanded or altered by any superior power.

But I intended here principally to make the following observation.

The fundamental principle of our government is, "The right of a people to give and grant their own money."—It is of no consequence, in this case, whether we enjoy this right in a proper manner or not. Most certainly we do not. It is, however, the *principle* on which our government, as a *free* government, is founded. The *spirit* of the constitution gives it us: and, however imperfectly enjoyed, we glory in it as our first and greatest blessing. It was an attempt to encroach upon this right, in a trifling instance, that produced the civil war in the reign of *Charles* the First. Ought not our brethren in *America* to enjoy this right as well as ourselves? Do the principles of the constitution give it us, but deny it to them? Or can we, with any decency, pretend that when we give to the king *their* money, we give him *our own?*(a)—What difference does it make, that in the time of *Charles the First* the attempt to take away this right was made by *one man:* but that, in the case of *America,* it is made by a body of men?

In a word. This is a war undertaken not only against the principles of our own constitution; but on purpose to destroy other similar constitutions in *America;* and to substitute in their room a military force. See page 12.—It is, therefore, a gross and flagrant violation of the constitution.

SECT. III.: *Of the Policy of the War with* America.

IN writing the present Section, I have entered upon a subject of the last importance, on which much has been said by other writers with great force, and in the ablest manner(b). But I am not willing to omit any topic which I think of great consequence, merely because it has already been discussed: And, with respect to this in particular, it will, I believe, be found that some of the observations on which I shall insist, have not been sufficiently attended to.

The object of this war has been often enough declared to be "maintaining the supremacy of this country over the colonies." I have already enquired how far reason and justice, the principles of Liberty, and the rights of humanity, entitle us to this supremacy. Setting aside, therefore, now all considerations of this kind, I would observe, that this supremacy is to be maintained, either merely *for its own sake,* or for the sake of some public interest connected with it] and dependent upon it.—If *for its own sake;* the only object of the war is the extension of dominion; and its only motive is the lost of power.—All government, even *within* a state, becomes tyrannical, as far as it is a needless and wanton exercise of power; or is carried farther than is absolutely necessary to preserve the peace and to secure the safety of the state. This is what an excellent writer calls GOVERNING TOO MUCH; and its effect must always be, weakening government by rendering it contemptible and odious.—Nothing can be of more importance, in governing distant provinces and adjusting the clashing interests of different societies, than attention to this remark. In these circumstances it is *particularly* necessary to make a sparing use of power, in order to preserve power.—Happy would it have been for *Great Britain,* had this been remembered by those who have lately conducted its affairs. But our policy has been of another kind. At the period when our authority should have been most concealed, it has been brought most in view; and, by a progression of violent measures, every one of which has increased distress, we have given the world reason to conclude, that we are acquainted with no other method of governing than *by force.*—What a shocking mistake?—If our object is power, we should have known better how to use it; and our rulers should have considered, that freemen will always revolt at the sight of a naked sword; and that the complicated affairs of a great kingdom, holding in subordination to it a multitude of distant communities, all jealous of their rights, and warmed with spirits as high as our own, require not only the most skilful, but the most cautious and tender management. The consequences of a different management we are now feeling. We see ourselves driven among rocks, and in danger of being lost.

There are the following reasons which seem to make it too probable, that the present contest with *America* is a contest for power only(*a*), abstracted from all the advantages connected with it.

1*st.* There is a love of power inherent in human nature; and it cannot be uncharitable to suppose that the nation in general, and the cabinet in particular, are too likely to be influenced by it. What can be more slattering than to look across the *Atlantic,* and to see in the boundless continent of *America,* increasing MILLIONS whom we have a right to order as we please, who hold their property at our disposal, and who have no other law than our will? With what complacency have we been used to talk of them as OURsubjects?—Is it not the interruption they now give to this pleasure? Is it not the opposition they make to our pride; and not any injury they have done us, that is the secret spring of our present animosity against them?—I wish all in this kingdom would examine themselves carefully on this point. Perhaps, they might find, that they have not known what spirit they are of.—Perhaps, they would become sensible, that it was a spirit of domination, more than a regard to the true interest of this country, that lately led so many of them, with such savage folly, to address the throne for the slaughter of their brethren in *America,* if they will not submit to them; and to make offers of their lives and fortunes for that purpose.—Indeed, I am persuaded, that, were pride and the lust of dominion exterminated from every heart among us, and the humility of Christians infused in their room, this quarrel would be soon ended.

2*dly*. Another reason for believing that this is a contest for power only is, that our ministers have frequently declared, that their object is not to draw a revenue from *America;* and that many of those who are warmest for continuing it, represent the *American trade* as of no great consequence.

]

But what deserves particular consideration here is, that this is a contest from which no advantages can possibly be derived.—Not a revenue: For the provinces of America, when desolated, will afford no revenue; or if they should, the expence of subduing them and keeping them in subjection will much exceed that revenue.—Not any of the advantages of trade: For it is a folly, next to insanity, to think trade can be promoted by impoverishing our customers, and fixing in their minds an everlasting abhorrence of us.—It remains, therefore, that this war can have no other object than the extension of power.— Miserable reflection!—To sheath our swords in the bowels of our brethren, and spread misery and ruin among a happy people, for no other end than to oblige them to acknowledge our supremacy. How horrid!—This is the cursed ambition that led a *Cæsar* and an *Alexander,* and many other mad conquerors, to attack peaceful communities, and to lay waste the earth.

But a worse principle than even this, influences some among us. Pride and the love of dominion are principles hateful enough; but blind resentment and the desire of revenge are infernal principles: And these, I am afraid, have no small share at present in guiding our public conduct.—One cannot help indeed being astonished at the virulence, with which some speak on the present occasion against the Colonies.—For, what have they done?—Have they crossed the ocean and invaded us? Have they attempted to take from us the fruits of our labour, and to overturn that form of government which we hold so sacred?—This cannot be pretended.—On the contrary. This is what we have done to them.—We have transported ourselves to their peaceful retreats, and employed our fleets and armies to stop up their ports, to destroy their commerce, to seize their effects, and to burn their towns. Would we but let them alone, and suffer them to enjoy in security their property and governments, instead of disturbing us, they would thank and bless us. And yet it is WE who imagine ourselves illused.—The truth is, we expected to find them a cowardly rabble who would lie quietly at our feet; and they have disappointed us. They have risen in their own defence, and repelled force by force. They deny the plenitude of our power over them; and insist upon being treated as free communities.—It is THIS that has provoked us; and kindled our governors into rage.

I hope I shall not here be understood to intimate, that *all*who promote this war are actuated by these principles. Some, I doubt not, are influenced by no other principle, than a regard to what they think the just authority of this country over its colonies, and to the unity and indivisibility of the British Empire. I wish such could be engaged to enter thoroughly into the enquiry, which has been the subject of the first part of this pamphlet; and to consider, particularly, how different a thing maintaining the authority of government *within* a state is from maintaining the authority of one people over another, already happy in the enjoyment of a government of their own. I wish farther they would consider, that the desire of maintaining authority is warrantable, only as far as it is the means of promoting some end, and doing some good; and that, before we resolve to spread famine and fire through a country in order to make it acknowledge our authority, we ought to be assured that great advantages will arise not only to ourselves, but to the country we wish to conquer.—That from the present contest no advantage to ourselves can arise, has been already shewn, and will presently be shewn more at large.—That no advantage to the Colonies can arise from it, need not, I hope, be shewn. It has however been asserted, that even *their* good is intended by this war. Many of us are persuaded, that they will be much happier under our government, than under any government of their own; and that their liberties will be safer when held for them by us, than when trusted in their own hands.—How kind is it thus to take upon us the trouble of judging for them what is most for their happiness? Nothing can be kinder except the resolution we have formed to exterminate them, if they will not submit to our judgment.—What] strange language have I sometimes heard? By an armed force we are now endeavouring to destroy the laws and governments of America; and yet I have heard it said, that we are endeavouring to support law and government there. We are insisting upon our right to levy contributions upon them; and to maintain this right, we are bringing upon them all the miseries a people can endure; and yet it is asserted, that we mean nothing but their security and happiness.

But I have wandered a little from the point I intended principally to insist upon in this section, which is, "the folly, in respect of policy, of the measures which have brought on this contest; and its pernicious and fatal tendency."

The following observations will, I believe, abundantly prove this.

1*st.* There are points which are likely always to suffer by discussion. Of this kind are most points of authority and prerogative; and the best policy is to avoid, as much as possible, giving any occasion for calling them into question.

The Colonies were at the beginning of this reign in the habit of acknowledging our authority, and of allowing us as much power over them as our interest required; and more, in some instances, than we could reasonably claim. This habit they would have retained: and had we, instead of imposing new burdens upon them, and increating their restraints, studied to promote their commerce, and to grant them new indulgences, they would have been always growing more attached to us. Luxury, and, together with it, their dependence upon us, and our influence(*a*) in their assemblies, would have increased, till in time perhaps they would have become as corrupt as ourselves; and we might have succeeded to our wishes in establishing our authority over them.—But, happily for them, we have chosen a different course. By exertions of authority which have alarmed them, they have been put upon examining into the grounds of all our claims, and forced to give up their luxuries, and to seek all their resources within themselves: And the issue is likely to prove the loss of *all* our authority over them, and of all the advantages connected with it. So little do men in power sometimes know how to preserve power; and so remarkably does the desire of extending dominion sometimes destroy it.—Mankind are naturally disposed to continue in subjection to that mode of government, be it what it will, under which they have been born and educated. Nothing rouses them into resistance but gross abuses, or some particular oppressions out of the road to which they have been used. And he who will examine the history of the world will find, there has generally been more reason for complaining that they have been too patient, than that they have been turbulent and rebellious.

Our governors, ever since I can remember, have been jealous that the Colonies, some time or other, would throw off their dependence. This jealousy was not founded on any of their acts or declarations. They have always, while at *peace* with us, disclaimed any such design; and they have continued to disclaim it since they have been at *war* with us. I have reason, indeed, to believe, that independency is, even at this moment, generally dreaded among them as a calamity to which they are in danger of being driven, in order to avoid a greater.—The jealousy I have mentioned, was, however, natural; and betrayed a secret opinion, that the subjection in which they were held was more than we could expect them always to endure. In such circumstances, all possible care should have been taken to give them no reason for discontent; and to preserve them in subjection, by keeping in that line of conduct to which custom had reconciled them, or at least never deviating from it, except with great caution; and particularly, by avoiding all direct attacks on their property and legislations. Had we done this, the different interests of so many states scattered over a vast continent, joined to our own prudence and moderation, would have enabled us to] maintain them in dependence for ages to come.—But instead of this, how have we acted?—It is in truth too evident, that our whole conduct, instead of being directed by that sound policy and foresight which in such circumstances were absolutely necessary, has been nothing (to say the best of it) but a series of the blindest rigour followed by retractation; a violence followed by concession; of mistake, weakness, and inconsistency.—A recital of a few facts, within every body's recollection, will fully prove this.

In the 6th of *George the Second,* an act was passed for imposing certain duties on all foreign spirits, melasses and sugars imported into the plantations. In this act, the duties imposed are said to be GIVEN and GRANTED by the Parliament to the King; and this is the first *American* act in which these words have been used. But notwithstanding this, as the act had the appearance of being only a regulation of trade, the colonies submitted to it; and a small direct revenue was drawn by it from them.—In the 4th of the present reign, many alterations were made in this act, with the declared purpose of making provision for raising a revenue in America. This alarmed the Colonies; and produced discontents and remonstrances which might have convinced our rulers this was tender ground, on which it became them to tread very gently.—There is, however, no reason to doubt but in time they would have sunk into a quiet submission to this revenue act, as being at worst only the exercise of a power which then they seem not to have thought much of contesting; I mean, the power of taxing them EXTERNALLY.—But before they had time to cool, a worse provocation was given them: and the STAMP-ACT was passed. This being an attempt to tax them INTERNALLY; and a direct attack on their property, by a power which would not suffer itself to be questioned; which eased *itself* by loading *them;* and to which it was impossible to six any bounds; they were thrown at once, from one end of the continent to the other, into resistance and rage.—Government, dreading the consequences, gave way; and the Parliament (upon a change of ministry) repealed the *Stamp-Act,* without requiring from them any recognition of its authority, or doing any more to preserve its dignity, than asserting, by the declaratory law, that it was possessed of full power and authority to make laws to bind them in all cases whatever.—Upon this, peace was restored; and, had no farther attempts of the same kind been made, they would undoubtedly have suffered us (as the people of *Ireland* have done) to enjoy quietly our declaratory law. They would have recovered their former habits of subjection; and our connection with them might have continued an increasing source of our wealth and glory.—But the spirit of despotism and avarice, always blind and restless, soon broke forth again. The scheme for drawing a revenue from *America,* by parliamentary taxation, was resumed; and in a little more than a year after the repeal of the *Stamp Act,* when all was peace, a third act was passed, imposing duties payable in *America* on tea, paper, glass, painters colours, &c.—This, as might have been expected, revived all the former heats; and the Empire was a second time threatened with the most dangerous commotions.—Government receded again; and the Parliament (under another change of ministry) repealed all the obnoxious duties, EXCEPT that upon tea. This exception was made in order to maintain a shew of dignity. But it was, in reality, sacrificing safety to pride; and leaving a splinter in the wound to produce a gangrene.—For some time, however, this relaxation answered its intended purposes. Our commercial intercourse with the Colonies was again recovered; and they avoided nothing but that tea which we had excepted in our repeal. In this state would things have remained, and even tea would perhaps in time have been gradually admitted, had not the evil genius of *Britain* stepped forth once more to embroil the Empire.

The *East India* company having fallen under difficulties, partly in consequence of the loss of the *American* market for tea, a scheme was formed for assisting them by an attempt to recover that market. With this view an act was] passed to enable them to export their tea to *America* free of all duties here, and subject only to 3d. per pound duty, payable in *America.* By this expedient they were enabled to offer it at a low price; and it was expected the consequence would prove that the Colonies would be tempted by it; a precedent gained for taxing them, and at the same time the company relieved. Ships were, therefore, fitted out; and large cargoes sent. The snare was too gross to escape the notice of the Colonies. They saw it, and spurned at it. They refused to admit the tea; and at BOSTON some persons in disguise buried it in the sea.— Had our governors in this case satisfied themselves with requiring a compensation from the province for the damage done, there is no doubt but it would have been granted. Or had they proceeded no farther in the infliction of punishment, than stopping up the port and destroying the trade of Boston, till compensation was made, the province might possibly have submitted, and a sufficient saving would have been gained for the honour of the nation. But having hitherto proceeded without wisdom, they observed now no bounds in their resentment. To the Boston port bill was added a bill which destroyed the chartered government of the province; a bill which withdrew from the jurisdiction of the province, persons who in particular cases should commit murder; and the *Quebec* bill. At the same time a strong body of troops was stationed at *Boston* to enforce obedience to these bills.

All who knew any thing of the temper of the Colonies saw that the effect of all this sudden accumulation of vengeance, would probably be not intimidating but exasperating them, and driving them into a general revolt. But our ministers had different apprehensions. They believed that the malecontents in the Colony of *Massachusett*'s were a small party, headed by a few factious men; that the majority of the people would take the side of government, as soon as they saw a force among them capable of supporting them; that, at worst, the Colonies in general would never make a common cause with this province; and that, the issue would prove, in a few months, order, tranquillity, and submission.—Every one of these apprehensions was falsified by the events that followed.

When the bills I have mentioned came to be carried into execution, the whole Province was thrown into confusion. Their courts of justice were shut up, and all government was dissolved. The commander in chief found it necessary to fortify himself in BOSTON; and the other Colonies immediately resolved to make a common cause with this Colony.

So strangely misinformed were our ministers, that this was all a surprise upon them. They took fright, therefore; and once more made an effort to retreat; but indeed the most ungracious one that can well be imagined. A proposal was sent to the Colonies, called Conciliatory; and the substance of which was, that if any of them would raise such sums as should be demanded of them by taxing themselves, the Parliament would forbear to tax them.—It will be scarcely believed, hereafter, that such a proposal could be thought conciliatory. It was only telling them; "If you will tax yourselves BY OUR ORDER, we will save "ourselves the trouble of taxing you."—They received the proposal as an insult; and rejected it with disdain.

At the time this concession was transmitted to *America,* open hostilities were not begun. In the sword our ministers thought they had still a resource which would immediately settle all disputes. They considered the people of *New-England* as nothing but a mob, who would be soon routed and forced into obedience. It was even believed, that a few thousands of our army might march through all *America,* and make all quiet wherever they went. Under this conviction our ministers did not dread urging the Province of *Massachusett's Bay* into rebellion, by ordering the army to seize their stores, and to take up some of their

leading men.—The attempt was made.—The people sled
immediately to arms, and repelled] the attack.—A
considerable part of the flower of the British army has been
destroyed.—Some of our best Generals, and the bravest of
our troops, are now disgracefully and miserably imprisoned
at *Boston*.—A horrid civil war is commenced;—And the
Empire is distracted and convulsed.

Can it be possible to think with patience of the policy that
has brought us into these circumstances? Did ever Heaven
punish the vices of a people more severely by darkening
their counsels? How great would be our happiness could
we now recal former times, and return to the policy of the
last reigns?—But those times are gone.—I will, however,
beg leave for a few moments to look back to them; and to
compare the ground we have left with that on which we
find ourselves. This must be done with deep regret; but it
forms a necessary part of my present design.

In those times our Colonies, foregoing every advantage
which they might derive from trading with foreign nations,
consented to send only to us whatever it was for our
interest to receive from them; and to receive only from us
whatever it was for our interest to send to them. They gave
up the power of making sumptuary laws and exposed
themselves to all the evils of an increasing and wasteful
luxury, because we were benefited by vending among them
the materials of it. The iron with which Providence had
blessed their country, they were required by laws, in which
they acquiesced, to transport hither, that our people might
be maintained by working it for them into nails, ploughs,
axes, &c. And, in several instances, even one Colony was
not allowed to supply any neighbouring Colonies with
commodities, which could be conveyed to them from
hence.—But they yielded much farther. They consented
that we should have the appointment of one branch of their

legislature. By recognizing as their King, a King resident among us and under our influence, they gave us a negative on all their laws. By allowing an appeal to us in their civil disputes, they gave us likewise the ultimate determination of all civil causes among them.—In short. They allowed us every power we could desire, except that of taxing them, and interfering in their internal legislations: And they had admitted precedents which, even in these instances, gave us no inconsiderable authority over them. By purchasing our goods they paid our taxes; and by allowing us to regulate their trade in any manner we thought most for our advantage, they enriched our merchants, and helped us to bear our growing burdens. They fought our battles with us. They gloried in their relation to us. All their gains centered among us; and they always spoke of this country and looked to it as their home.

Such WAS the state of things.—What is it now?

Not contented with a degree of power, sufficient to satisfy any reasonable ambition, we have attempted to extend it.— Not contented with drawing from them a large revenue *indirectly,* we have endeavoured to procure one *directly* by an authoritative seizure; and, in order to gain a pepper-corn in this way, have chosen to hazard millions, acquired by the peaceable intercourse of trade.— Vile policy! What a scourge is government so conducted?—Had we never deserted our old ground: Had we nourished and favoured *America,* with a view to commerce, instead of considering it as a country to be governed: Had we, like a liberal and wife people, rejoiced to see a multitude of free states branched forth from ourselves, all enjoying independent legislatures similar to our own: Had we aimed at binding them to us only by the tyes of affection and interest; and contented ourselves with a moderate power rendered durable by being lenient and

49

friendly, an umpire in their differences, an aid to them in improving their own free governments, and their common bulwark against the assaults of foreign enemies: Had this, I say, been our policy and temper; there is nothing so great or happy that we might not have expected. With their increase our strength would have increased. A growing surplus in the revenue might have been gained, which, invariably applied to the gradual discharge of the national debt, would]have delivered us from the ruin with which it threatens us. The Liberty of *America* might have preserved our Liberty; and, under the direction of a patriot king or wise minister, proved the means of restoring to us our almost lost constitution. Perhaps, in time, we might also have been brought to see the necessity of carefully watching and restricting our paper-credit: And thus we might have regained safety; and, in union with our Colonies, have been more than a match for every enemy, and risen to a situation of honour and dignity never before known amongst mankind.—But I am forgetting myself— Our Colonies are likely to be lost for ever. Their love is turned into hatred; and their respect for our government into resentment and abhorrence.—We shall see more distinctly what a calamity this is, and the observations I have now made will be confirmed, by attending to the following facts.

Our American Colonies, particularly the Northern ones, have been for some time in the very happiest state of society; or, in that middle state of civilization, between its first rude and its last refined and corrupt state. Old countries consist, generally, of three classes of people; a GENTRY; a YEOMANRY;and a PEASANTRY. The Colonies consist only of a body of YEOMANRY(*a*) supported by agriculture, and all independent, and nearly upon a level; in consequence of which, joined to a boundless extent of country, the means of subsistence are procured without difficulty, and the temptations to wickedness are so inconsiderable, that executions(b) are seldom known among them. From hence arises an encouragement to population so great, that in some of the Colonies they double their own number in fifteen years; in others, in eighteen years; and in all, taken one with another, in twenty-five years.—Such an increase was, I believe, never before known. It demonstrates that they must live at their ease; and be free from those cares, oppressions, and diseases which depopulate and ravage luxurious states.

With the population of the Colonies has increased their trade; but much faster, on account of the gradual introduction of luxury among them.—In 1723 the exports to *Pensylvania* were 16,000 l.—In 1742 they were 75,295 l.—In 1757 they were increased to 268,426 l. and in 1773 to half a million.

The exports to all the Colonies in 1744 were 640,114 l.—In 1758, they were increased to 1,832,948 l. and in 1773, to three millions.(c) And the probability is, that, had it not been for the discontents among the Colonies since the year 1764, our trade with them would have been this year double to what it was in 1773; and that in a few years more, it would not have been possible for the whole kingdom, though consisting only of manufacturers, to supply the American demand.

This trade, it should be considered, was not only thus an increasing trade; but it was a trade in which we had no rivals; a trade certain, constant, and uninterrupted; and which, by the shipping employed in it, and the naval stores supplied by it, contributed greatly to the support of that navy which is our chief national strength.—Viewed in these lights it was an object unspeakably important. But it will appear still more so if we view it in its connexions and

dependencies. It is well known, that our trade
with *Africa*and the *West-Indies*] cannot easily subsist
without it. And, upon the whole, it is undeniable, that it has
been one of the main springs of our opulence and
splendour; and that we have, in a great measure, been
indebted to it for our ability to bear a debt so much heavier,
than that which, fifty years ago, the wisest men thought
would necessarily sink us.

This inestimable prize, and all the advantages connected
with *America,* we are now throwing away. Experience
alone can shew what calamities must follow. It will indeed
be astonishing if this kingdom can bear such a loss without
dreadful consequences.—These consequences have been
amply represented by others; and it is needless to enter into
any account of them—At the time we shall be seeing
them—The Empire dismembered; the blood of thousands
shed in an unrighteous quarrel; our strength exhausted; our
merchants breaking; our manufacturers starving; our debts
increasing; the revenue sinking; the funds tottering; and all
the miseries of a public bankruptcy impending—At such
a *crisis* should our natural enemies, eager for our ruin, seize
the opportunity—The apprehension is too distressing.—Let
us view this subject in another light.

On this occasion, particular attention should be given to the
present SINGULAR situation of this kingdom. This is a
circumstance of the utmost importance; and as I am afraid
it is not much considered, I will beg leave to give a distinct
account of it.

At the REVOLUTION, the *specie* of the kingdom amounted,
according to(a) *Davenant*'s account, to eighteen millions
and a half.—From the ACCESSION to the year 1772, there
were coined at the mint, near 29 millions of gold; and in ten
years only of this time, or from January 1759 to January

1769, there were coined eight millions and a half.(*b*) But it has appeared lately, that the gold specie now left in the kingdom is no more than about twelve millions and a half.—Not so much as half a million of *Silver specie* has been coined these sixty years; and it cannot be supposed, that the quantity of it now in circulation exceeds two or three millions. The whole specie of the kingdom, therefore, is probably at this time about(*c*) fourteen or fifteen millions. Of this several millions must be hoarded at the *Bank.*—Our circulating *specie,* therefore, appears to be greatly decreased. But our wealth, or the quantity of money in the kingdom, is greatly increased. This is paper to a vast amount, issued in almost every corner of the kingdom; and, particularly, by the BANK OF ENGLAND. While this paper maintains its credit it answers all the purposes of specie, and is in all respects the same with money.

Specie represents some real value in goods or commodities. On the contrary; paper represents nothing immediately but specie. It is a promise or obligation, which the emitter brings himself under to pay a given sum in coin; and it owes its currency to the credit of the emitter; or to an opinion that he is able to make good his engagement; and that the sum specified may be received upon being demanded.—Paper, therefore, represents coin; and coin represents real value. That is, the one is a *sign* of wealth. The other is a *sign* of that *sign.*—But farther. Coin is an *universal* sign of wealth, and will procure it every where. It will bear any alarm, and stand any shock.—On the contrary. Paper, owing its currency to opinion, has only a local and imaginary value. It can stand no shock. It is destroyed by the approach of danger; or even the *suspicion* of danger.

In short. Coin is the basis of our paper-credit; and were it either all destroyed, or were only the quantity of it reduced beyond a certain limit, the] paper circulation of the kingdom would fink at once. But, were our paper destroyed, the coin would not only remain, but rise in value, in proportion to the quantity of paper destroyed.

From this account it follows, that as far as, in any circumstances, specie is not to be procured in exchange for paper, it represents *nothing,* and is worth *nothing.*—The specie of this kingdom is inconsiderable, compared with the amount of the paper circulating in it. This is generally believed; and, therefore, it is natural to enquire how its currency is supported.—The answer is easy. It is supported in the same manner with all other bubbles. Were all to demand specie in exchange for their notes, payment could not be made; but, at the same time that this is known, every one trusts, that no alarm producing such a demand will happen, while he holds the paper he is possessed of; and that if it should happen, he will stand a chance for being first paid; and this makes him easy. And it also makes all with whom he trafficks easy.—But let any events happen which threaten danger; and every one will become diffident. A run will take place; and a bankruptcy follow.

This is an account of what *has* often happened in *private*credit. And it is also an account of what *will* (if no change of measures takes place) happen some time or other in *public*credit. The description I have given of our papercirculation implies, that nothing can be more delicate or hazardous. It is an immense fabrick, with its head in the clouds, that is continually trembling with every adverse blast and every fluctuation of trade; and which, like the baseless fabrick of a vision, may in a moment vanish, and leave no wreck behind.—The destruction of a few books at the *Bank;* an improvement in the art of forgery; the landing of a body of *French* troops on our coasts; insurrections threatening a revolution in government; or any events that

54

should produce a general panic, however groundless, would at once annihilate it, and leave us without any other medium of traffic, than a quantity of *specie* scarcely equal in amount to the money now drawn from the public by the taxes. It would, therefore, become impossible to pay the taxes. The revenue would fail. Near a hundred and forty millions of property would be destroyed. The whole frame of government would fall to pieces; and a state of nature would take place.—What a dreadful situation? It has never had a parallel among mankind; except at one time in *France* after the establishment there of the Royal *Mississippi* Bank. In 1720 this bank broke(*a*); and, after involving for some time the whole kingdom in a golden dream, spread through it in one day, desolation and ruin.—The distress atrending such an event, in this free country, would be greater than it was in *France.* Happily for that kingdom, they have shot this gulph. Paper-credit has never since recovered itself there; and their circulating cash consists now all of solid coin, amounting, I am informed, to no less a sum than 1500 millions of *Livres;* or near 67 millions of pounds sterling. This gives them unspeakable advantages; and, joined to that quick reduction of their debts which is inseparable(*b*) from their nature, places them on a ground of safety which we have reason to admire and envy.

These are subjects on which I should have chosen to be silent, did I not think it necessary, that this country should be apprized and warned of the danger] which threatens it. This danger is created chiefly by the national debt. High taxes are necessary to support a great public debt; and a large supply of cash is necessary to support high taxes. This cash we owe to our paper; and, in proportion to our paper, must be the productiveness of our taxes.—King William's wars drained the kingdom of its specie. This sunk the revenue, and distressed government. In 1694 the BANK was established; and the kingdom was provided with a substitute for specie. The taxes became again productive. The revenue rose; and government was relieved.—Ever since that period our paper and taxes have been increasing together, and supporting one another; and one reason, undoubtedly, of the late increase in the productiveness of our taxes has been the increase of our paper.

Was there no public debt, there would be no occasion for half the present taxes. Our paper-circulation might be reduced. The balance of trade would turn in our favour. Specie would flow in upon us. The quantity of property destroyed by a failure of paper-credit (should it in such circumstances happen) would be 140 millions less; and, therefore, the shock attending it would be *tolerable*. But, in the present state of things, whenever any calamity or panic shall produce such a failure, the shock attending it will be *intolerable*.—May Heaven soon raise up for us some great statesman who shall see these things; and enter into effectual measures, if not now too late, for extricating and preserving us!

Public banks are, undoubtedly, attended with great conveniencies. But they also do great harm; and, if their emissions are not restrained, and conducted with great wisdom, they may prove the most pernicious of all institutions; not only, by substituting *fictitious* for *real* wealth; by increasing luxury; by raising the prices of provisions; by concealing an unfavourable balance of trade; and by rendering a kingdom incapable of bearing any *internal* tumults or *external* attacks, without the danger of a dreadful convulsion: but, particularly, by becoming instruments in the hands of ministers of state to increase their influence, to lessen their dependence on the people, and to keep up a delusive shew of public prosperity, when perhaps, ruin may

be near. There is, in truth, nothing that a government may not do with such a mine at its command as a public Bank, while it can maintain its credit; nor, therefore, is there any thing more likely to
be IMPROPERLY and DANGEROUSLY used.—But to return to what may be more applicable to our own state at present.

Among the causes that may produce a failure of paper-credit, there are two which the present quarrel with *America*calls upon us particularly to consider.—The first is, "An unfavourable balance of trade." This, in proportion to the degree in which it takes place, must turn the course of foreign exchange against us; raise the price of bullion; and carry off our specie. The danger to which this would expose us is obvious; and it has been much increased by the new coinage of the gold specie which begun in 1772. Before this coinage, the greatest part of our gold coin being light, but the same in currency as if it had been heavy, always remained in the kingdom. But, being now full weight, whenever a wrong balance of foreign trade alters the course of exchange, and gold in *coin* becomes of less value than in *bullion,* there is reason to fear, that it will be melted down in such great quantities, and exported so fast, as in a little time to leave none behind;(a) the consequence of which must prove, that the whole] superstructure of paper-credit, now supported by it, will break down.—The only remedy, in such circumstances, is an increase of coinage at the mint. But this will operate too slowly; and, by raising the price of bullion, will only increase the evil.— It is the *Bank* that at such a time must be the immediate sufferer: For it is from thence that those who want coin for any purpose will always draw it.

For many years before 1772, the price of gold in *bullion* had been from 2 to 3 or 4 *per cent.* higher than in *coin.* This was a temptation to melt down and export the

57

coin, which could not be resisted. Hence arose a demand
for it on the BANK;and, consequently, the necessity of
purchasing bullion at a loss for a new coinage. But the
more coin the Bank procured in this way, the lower its price
became in comparison with that of bullion, and the faster it
vanished; and consequently, the more necessary it became
to coin again, and the greater loss fell upon the Bank.—Had
things continued much longer in this train, the
consequences might have proved very serious. I am by no
means sufficiently informed to be able to assign the causes
which have produced the change that happened in 1772.
But, without doubt, the state of things that took place
before that year, must be expected to return. The
fluctuations of trade, in its best state, render this
unavoidable. But the contest with our Colonies has a
tendency to bring it on soon; and to increase unspeakably
the distress attending it.

All know that the balance of trade with them is greatly in
our favour;(a) and that this balance is paid partly by direct
remittances of bullion; and partly by circuitous remittances
through *Spain, Portugal, Italy,* &c. which diminish the
balance against us with these countries.—During the last
year, they have been employed in paying their debts,
without adding to them; and their exportations and
remittances for that purpose have contributed to render the
general balance of trade more favourable to us, and, also,
(in conjunction with the late operations of the Bank) to
keep up our funds. These remittances are now ceased; and a
year or two will determine, if this contest goes on, how far
we can sustain such a loss without suffering the
consequences I have described.

The second event, ruinous to our paper circulation, which
may arise from our rupture with *America,* is a deficiency in
the revenue. As a failure of our paper would destroy the

58

revenue, so a failure of the revenue, or any considerable diminution of it, would destroy our paper. The BANK is the support of our paper; and the support of the BANK is the credit of government. Its principal securities, are a capital of near eleven millions lent to government; and money continually advanced to a vast amount on the Land-tax, Sinking fund, Exchequer Bills, Navy Bills, &c. Should, therefore, deficiencies in the revenue bring government under any difficulties, all these securities would lose their value, and the *Bank* and Government, and all private and public credit, would fall together.—Let any one here imagine, what would probably follow, were it but suspected by the public in general, that the taxes were so fallen, as not to produce enough to pay the interest of the public debts, besides bearing the *ordinary* expences of the nation; and that, in order to supply the deficiency and to hide the calamity, it had been necessary in any one year to anticipate the taxes, and to borrow of the Bank.—In such circumstances I can scarcely doubt, but an alarm would] spread of the most dangerous tendency.—The next foreign war, should it prove *half* as expensive as the last, will probably occasion such a deficiency; and bring our affairs to that crisis towards which they have been long tending.—But the war with *America* has a greater tendency to do this; and the reason is, that it affects our resources more; and is attended more with the danger of internal disturbances.

Some have made the proportion of our trade depending on *North America* to be near ONE HALF. A moderate computation makes it a THIRD.(*a*) Let it, however, be supposed to be only a FOURTH. I will venture to say, this is a proportion of our foreign trade, the loss of which, when it comes to be selt, will be found insupportable.—In the article of *Tobacco* alone it will cause a deduction from the *Customs* of at least 300,000 *l per ann.*(*b*) including the

59

duties paid on foreign commodities purchased by the exportation of tobacco. Let the whole deduction from the revenue be supposed to be only half a million. This alone is more than the kingdom can at present bear, without having recourse to additional taxes in order to defray the common and necessary expences of peace. But to this must be added a deduction from the produce of the *Excises,* in consequence of the increase of the poor, of the difficulties of our merchants and manufacturers, of less national wealth, and a retrenchment of luxury. There is no possibility of knowing to what these deductions may amount. When the evils producing them begin, they will proceed rapidly; and they may end in a general wreck before we are aware of any danger.

In order to give a clearer view of this subject, I will in an Appendix, state particularly the national expenditure and income for eleven years, from 1764 to 1774. From that account it will appear, that the money drawn every year from the public by the taxes, falls but little short of a sum equal to the whole *specie* of the kingdom; and that, notwithstanding the late increase in the productiveness of the taxes, the whole surplus of the national income has not exceeded 320,000 l. *per ann.*(c) This is a surplus so inconsiderable as to be scarcely sufficient to guard against the deficiencies arising from the common fluctuations of foreign trade, and of home consumption. It
is NOTHING when considered as the only fund we have for paying off a debt of near 140 millions.—Had we continued in a state of profound peace, it could not have admitted of any diminution. What then must follow, when one of the most profitable branches of our trade is destroyed; when a THIRD of the Empire is lost; when an addition of many millions is made to the public debt; and when, at the same time, perhaps, some millions are taken away from the revenue?—I shudder at this prospect.—A KINGDOM, ON AN

SECT. IV.: *Of the Honour of the Nation as affected by the War with* America.

ONE of the pleas for continuing the contest
with *America,* is "That our honour is engaged; and that we
cannot now recede without the most humiliating
concessions."

With respect to this, it is proper to observe, that a
distinction should be made between the nation, and its
rulers. It is melancholy that there should be ever ן any
ıeason for making such a distinction. A government is, or
ought to be, nothing but an institution for collecting and for
carrying into execution the will of the people. But so far is
this from being in general the fact, that the measures of
government, and the sense of the people, are sometimes in
direct opposition to one another; nor does it *often* happen
that any certain conclusion can be drawn from the one to
the other.—I will not pretend to determine, whether, in the
present instance, the dishonour attending a retreat would
belong to the nation at large, or only to the persons in
power who guide its affairs. Let it be granted, though
probably far from true, that the majority of the kingdom
savour the present measures. No good argument could be
drawn from hence against receding. The disgrace to which
a kingdom must submit by making concessions, is nothing
to that of being the aggressors in an unrighteous quarrel;
and dignity, in such circumstances, consists in retracting
freely, speedily, and magnanimously.—For, (to adopt, on
this occasion, words which I have heard applied to this very
purpose, in a great assembly, by a peer to whom this
kingdom has often looked as its deliverer, and whose ill

state of health at this awful moment of public danger every friend to *Britain* must deplore) to adopt, I say, the words of this great man, "RECTITUDE IS DIGNITY. OPPRESSION ONLY IS MEANNESS; AND JUSTICE, HONOUR."

I will add, that PRUDENCE, no less than true HONOUR, requires us to retract. For the time may come when, if it is not done voluntarily, we may be *obliged* to do it; and find ourselves under a necessity of granting that to our distresses, which we now deny to equity and humanity, and the prayers of *America*. The possibility of this appears plainly from the preceding pages; and should it happen, it will bring upon us disgrace indeed, disgrace greater than the worst rancour can wish to see accumulated on a kingdom already too much dishonoured.—Let the reader think here what we are doing.—A nation, once the protector of Liberty in distant countries, and the scourge of tyranny, changed into an enemy to Liberty, and engaged in endeavouring to reduce to servitude its own brethren.—A great and enlightened nation, not content with a controuling power over millions of people which gave it every reasonable advantage, insisting upon such a supremacy over them as would leave them nothing they could call their own, and carrying desolation and death among them for disputing it.—What can be more ignominious?—How have we felt for the brave *Corsicans,* in their struggle with the *Genoese,* and afterwards with the *French* government? Did GENOA or FRANCE want more than an absolute command over their property and legislations; or the power of binding them in all cases whatsoever?—
The *Corsicans* had been subject to the *Genoese;* but, finding it difficult to keep them in subjection, they CEDED them to the *French.*—All such cessions of one people by another are disgraceful to human nature. But if our claims are just, may not we also, if we please, CEDE the Colonies to *France?*—There is, in truth, no other difference

between these two cases than that the *Corsicans* were not descended from the people who governed them, but that the *Americans* are.

There are some who seem to be sensible, that the authority of one country over another, cannot be distinguished from the servitude of one country to another; and that unless different communities, as well as different parts of the same community, are united by an equal representation, all such authority is inconsistent with the principles of Civil Liberty. But they except the case of the Colonies and *Great Britain;* because the Colonies are communities which have branched forth from, and which, therefore, as they think, belong to *Britain.* Had the Colonies been communities of *foreigners,* over whom we wanted to acquire dominion, or even to extend a dominion before acquired, they are ready to admit that their resistance would have been just.— In my opinion, this is the same with saying, that the Colonies ought to be worse off than the rest of mankind, because they are our own *Brethren.*

]

Again. The United Provinces of *Holland* were once subject to the *Spanish* monarchy; but, provoked by the violation of their charters; by levies of money, without their consent; by the introduction of Spanish troops among them; by innovations in their antient modes of government; and the rejection of their petitions, they were driven to that resistance which we and all the world have ever since admired; and which has given birth to one of the greatest and happiest Republics that ever existed.—Let any one read also, the history of the war which the *Athenians,* from a thirst of Empire, made on the *Syracusans* in *Sicily,* a people derived from the same origin with them; and let

him, if he can, avoid rejoicing in the defeat of
the *Athenians.*

Let him, likewise, read the account of the social war among
the Romans. The allied states of *Italy* had sought the battles
of *Rome,* and contributed by their valour and treasure to its
conquests and grandeur. They claimed, therefore, the rights
of Roman citizens, and a share with them in legislation.
The Romans, disdaining to make those their *fellow-
citizens,* whom they had always looked upon as
their *subjects,* would not comply; and a war followed, the
most horrible in the annals of mankind, which ended in the
ruin of the Roman Republic. The feelings of
every *Briton* in this case must force him to approve the
conduct of the Allies, and to condemn the proud and
ungrateful Romans.

But not only is the present contest with *America* thus
disgraceful to us, because inconsistent with our own
feelings in similar cases; but also because condemned by
our own practice in former times. The Colonies are
persuaded that they are fighting for Liberty. We see them
sacrificing to this persuasion every private advantage. If
mistaken, and though guilty of irregularities, they should be
pardoned by a people whose ancestors have given them so
many examples of similar conduct. ENGLAND should
venerate the attachment of Liberty amidst all its excesses;
and, instead of indignation or scorn, it would be most
becoming them, in the present instance, to declare their
applause, and to say to the Colonies—"We excuse your
mistakes. We admire your spirit. It is the spirit that has
more than once saved *ourselves.* We aspire to no dominion
over you. We understand the rights of men too well to think
of taking from you the inestimable privilege of governing
yourselves; and, instead of employing our power for any
such purpose, we offer it to you as a friendly and guardian

power, to be a mediator in your quarrels; a protection against your enemies; and an aid to you in establishing a plan of Liberty that shall make you great and happy. In return, we ask nothing but your gratitude and your commerce."

This would be a language worthy of a brave and enlightened nation. But alas! it often happens in the *Political World* as it does in *Religion,* that the people who cry out most vehemently for Liberty to themselves are the most unwilling to grant it to others.

One of the most violent enemies of the Colonies has pronounced them "all Mr. Locke's disciples."—Glorious title!—How shameful is it to make war against them for that reason?

But farther. This war is disgraceful on account of the persuasion which led to it, and under which it has been undertaken. The general cry was last winter, that the people of NEW ENGLAND were a body of cowards, who would at once be reduced to submission by a hostile look from our troops. In this light were they held up to public derision in both Houses of Parliament; and it was this persuasion that, probably, induced a Nobleman of the first weight in the state to recommend, at the passing of the *Boston Port Bill,* coercive measures; hinting at the same time, that the *appearance* of hostilities would be sufficient, and that all would be soon over, SINE CLADE.—Indeed no one can doubt, but that had it been believed some time ago, that the people of *America* were brave, more care would have been taken not to provoke them.

Again. The manner in which this war has been hitherto conducted, renders it still more disgraceful.—English valour being thought insufficient to subdue] the Colonies, the laws and religion of *France* were established in *Canada,* on purpose to obtain the power of bringing upon them from thence an army of *French Papists.* The wild *Indians* and their own Slaves have been instigated to attack them; and attempts have been made to gain the assistance of a large body of *Russians.*—With like views, *German* troops have been hired; and the defence of our Forts and Garrisons trusted in their hands.

These are measures which need no comment. The last of them, in particular, having been carried into execution without the consent of parliament, threatens us with imminent danger; and shews that we are in the way to lose even the *Forms* of the constitution.—If, indeed, our ministers can at any time, without leave, not only send away the national troops, but introduce *foreign* troops in their room, we lie entirely at mercy; and we have every thing to dread.

SECT. V.: *Of the Probability of Succeeding in the War with* America.

LET us next consider how far there is a possibility of succeeding in the present war.

Our own people, being unwilling to enlist, and the attempts to procure armies of *Russians, Indians,* and *Canadians* having miscarried; the utmost force we can employ, including foreigners, does not exceed, if I am rightly informed, 30,000 effective men. Let it, however, be called 40,000. This is the force that is to conquer half a million *at least*(a) of determined men fighting on their own ground, within fight of their houses and families, and for that sacred blessing of Liberty, without which man is a beast, and government a curse. All history proves, that in such a situation, a handful is a match for millions.

In the *Netherlands,* a few states thus circumstanced, withstood, for thirty years, the whole force of the Spanish monarchy, when at its zenith; and at last humbled its pride, and emancipated themselves from its tyranny.—The citizens of SYRACUSE also, thus circumstanced, withstood the whole power of the *Athenians,* and almost ruined them.—The same happened in the contest between the house of *Austria,* and the cantons(b) of *Switzerland.*—There is in this case an infinite difference between attacking and being attacked; between fighting to *destroy,* and fighting to *preserve,* or *acquire* Liberty.—Were we, therefore, capable of employing a *land* force against *America* equal to its own, there would be little probability of success. But to think of conquering that whole continent with 30,000 or 40,000 men to be transported across the *Atlantic,* and fed from hence, and incapable of being recruited after any defeat.—This is indeed a folly so great, that language does not afford a name for it.

With respect to our naval force, could it sail at land as it does at sea, much might be done with it; but as that is impossible, *little* or *nothing* can be done with it, which will not hurt *ourselves* more than the *Colonists.*—Such of their maritime towns as they cannot guard against our fleets, and have not been already destroyed, they are determined either to give up to our resentment, or(c) destroy themselves: The consequence of which will be, that these towns will be rebuilt in safer situations; and that we shall lose some of the principal pledges by which we have hitherto held them in subjection.—As to their trade; having all the necessaries and the chief conveniencies of life within themselves, they have no dependence upon it; and the loss of it will do them unspeakable good, by preserving] them from the evils of luxury and the temptations of wealth; and keeping them in that state of virtuous simplicity which is the greatest happiness. I know that I am now speaking the sense of some of the wisest men in America. It has been long their wish that *Britain* would shut up all their ports. They will rejoice, particularly, in the last restraining act. It might have happened, that the people would have grown weary of their agreements not to export or import. But this act will oblige them to keep these agreements; and confirm their unanimity and zeal. It will also furnish them with a reason for confiscating the estates of all the friends of our government among them, and for employing their sailors, who would have been otherwise idle, in making reprisals on British property. Their ships, before useless, and consisting of many hundreds, will be turned into ships of war; and all that attention, which they have hitherto confined to trade, will be employed in fitting out a naval force for their own defence; and thus the way will be prepared for their becoming, much sooner than they would otherwise have been, a great maritime power. This act of parliament, therefore, crowns the folly of all our late measures.—None who know me, can believe me to be disposed to superstition. Perhaps, however, I am not in the present instance, free from this weakness.—I fancy I see in these measures something that cannot be accounted for merely by human ignorance. I am inclined to think, that the hand of Providence is in them working to bring about some great ends.—But this leads me to one consideration more, which I cannot help offering to the publick, and which appears to me in the highest degree important.

In this hour of tremendous danger, it would become us to turn our thoughts to Heaven. This is what our brethren in the Colonies are doing. From one end of *North America* to the other, they are FASTING and PRAYING. But what are we doing?—Shocking thought! we are ridiculing them as *Fanatics,* and scoffing at religion.—We are running wild after pleasure, and forgetting every thing serious and decent at *Masquerades.*—We are gambling in gaming houses; trafficking for Boroughs; perjuring ourselves at Elections; and selling ourselves for places.—Which side then is Providence likely to favour?

In *America* we see a number of rising states in the vigour of youth, inspired by the noblest of all passions, the passion for being free; and animated by piety.—*Here* we see an old state, great indeed, but inflated and irreligious; enervated by luxury; encumbered with debts; and hanging by a thread.—Can any one look without pain to the issue? May we not expect calamities that shall recover
to *reflection* (perhaps
to *devotion)* our *Libertines* and *Atheists?*

Is our cause such as gives us reason to ask God to bless it?—Can we in the face of Heaven declare, "that we are not the aggressors in this war; and that we mean by it, not to acquire or even preserve dominion for its own sake; not conquest, or Empire, or the gratification of resentment; but solely to deliver ourselves from oppression; to gain reparation for injury; and to defend ourselves against men who would plunder or kill us?"—Remember, reader, whoever thou art, that there are no other just causes of war; and that blood spilled, with any other views, must some time or other be accounted for.—But not to expose myself by saying more in this way. I will now beg leave to recapitulate some of the arguments I have used; and to deliver the feelings of my heart in a brief, but earnest address to my countrymen.

I am hearing it continually urged—"Are they not our subjects."—The plain answer is, they are not your subjects. The people of *America* are no more the subjects of the people of *Britain,* than the people of *Yorkshire* are the subjects of the people of *Middlesex.* They are your *fellow-subjects.*

"But *we* are taxed; and why should not *they* be taxed?"—*You*are taxed by yourselves. They insist on the same privilege.—They are taxed to support their own governments; and they help also to pay your taxes by purchasing] your manufactures, and giving you a monopoly of their trade. Must they maintain *two* governments? Must they submit to be *triple* taxed?—Has your moderation in taxing yourselves been such as encourages them to trust you with the power of taxing them?

"But they will not obey the *Parliament* and the *Laws."*—Say rather, they will not obey *your* Parliament and *your* laws. Their reason is: They have no voice in your Parliament. They have no share in making(a) your laws.—"Neither have *most*of us."—Then you so far want Liberty; and your language is, "*We* are not free; Why will *they* be free?"—But *many* of you have a voice in parliament; *None* of them have. *All* your freehold land is represented: But not a foot of *their* land is represented. At worst, therefore, you can be only enslaved *partially.*—They would be enslaved *totally.*—They are governed by parliaments chosen by themselves, and by legislatures similar to yours. Why will you disturb them in the enjoyment of a blessing so invaluable? Is it reasonable to insist, that your discretion alone shall be their law; that they shall have no constitutions of government, except such as you shall be pleased to give them; and no property except such as your parliament shall be pleased to leave them?—What is your parliament?—Powerful indeed and respectable: But is there not a growing intercourse between it and the court? Does it awe ministers of state as it once did?—Instead of contending for a controuling power over the governments of *America,* should you not think more of watching and reforming your own?—Suppose the worst. Suppose, in opposition to all their own declarations, that the Colonists are now aiming at independence.—"If they can subsist without you;" is it to be wondered at? Did there ever exist a *community,* or even an *individual,* that would not do the same?—"If they *cannot* subsist without you;" let them alone. They will soon come back.—"If you cannot subsist without them;" reclaim them by(b) kindness; engage them by moderation and equity. It is madness to resolve to butcher them. This will make them detest and avoid you for ever. Free men are not to be governed by force; or dragooned into compliance. If capable of bearing to be so treated, it is a disgrace to be connected with them.

"If *they* can subsist without you; and also *you* without them," the attempt to subjugate them by confiscating their effects, burning their towns, and ravaging their territories, is a wanton exertion of cruel ambition, which, however common it has been among mankind, deserves to be called by harder names than I chuse to apply to it.—Suppose such an attempt was to be succeeded: Would it not be a fatal preparation for subduing yourselves? Would not the disposal of *American* places, and the distribution of an *American*revenue, render that influence of the crown irresistible, which has already stabbed your liberties?

]

Turn your eyes to *India:* There more has been done than is now attempted in *America.* There ENGLISHMEN, actuated by the love of plunder and the spirit of conquest, have depopulated whole kingdoms, and ruined millions of innocent people by the most infamous oppression and rapacity.—The justice of the nation has slept over these enormities. Will the justice of Heaven sleep?—Are we not now execrated on both sides of the globe?

With respect to the Colonists; it would be folly to pretend they are faultless. They were running fast into our vices. But this quarrel gives them a salutary check: And it may be permitted on purpose to favour them, and in them the rest of mankind; by making way for establishing, in an extensive country possessed of every advantage, a plan of government, and a growing power that shall astonish the world, and under which every subject of human enquiry shall be open to free discussion, and the friends of Liberty, in every quarter of the globe, find a safe retreat from civil and spiritual tyranny.—I hope, therefore, our brethren in *America* will forgive their enemies. It is certain that *they know not what they are doing.*

CONCLUSION.

HAVING said so much of the war with America, and particularly of the danger with which it threatens us, it may be expected that I should propose some method of escaping from this danger, and of restoring this once happy Empire to a state of peace and security.—Various plans of pacification have been proposed; and some of them, by persons so distinguished by their rank and merit, as to be above my applause. But till there is more of a disposition to attend to such plans; they cannot, I am afraid, be of any great service. And there is too much reason to apprehend, that nothing but calamity will bring us to repentance and wisdom.—In order, however, to complete my design in these observations, I will take the liberty to lay before the public the following sketch of one of the plans just referred to, as it was opened before the holidays to the house of Lords by the *Earl of Shelburne,* who, while he held the seals of the Southern Department, with the business of the

Colonies annexed, possessed their confidence, without ever compromising the authority of this country; a confidence which discovered itself by peace among themselves, and duty and submission to the Mother-country. I hope I shall not take an unwarrantable liberty, if, on this occasion, I use his Lordship's own words, as nearly as I have been able to collect them.

"Meet the Colonies on their own ground, in the last petition from the Congress to the king. The surest, as well as the most dignified mode of proceeding for this country.— Suspend all hostilities—Repeal the acts which immediately distress America, namely, the last restraining act,—the charter act,—the act for the more impartial administration of justice;—and the Quebec act.—All the other acts (the custom house act, the post office act, &c.) leave to a temperate revisal.—There will be found much matter which both countries may wish repealed. *Some* which can never be given up, the principle being that regulation of trade for the common good of the Empire, which forms our *Palladium. Other* matter which is fair subject of mutual accommodation.—Prescribe the most explicit acknowledgement of your right of regulating commerce in its most extensive sense; if the petition and other public acts of the Colonies have not already, by their declarations and acknowledgements, left it upon a sufficiently secure foundation.—Besides the power of regulating the general commerce of the Empire, something further might be expected; provided a due and tender regard were had to the means] and abilities of the several provinces, as well as to those fundamental, unalienable rights of *Englishmen,* which no father can surrender on the part of his son, no representative on the part of his elector, no generation on the part of the succeeding one; the right of judging not only of the *mode* of raising, but the *quantum,* and the appropriation of such aids as they shall grant.—To be more explicit; the debt of *England,* without entering into invidious distinctions how it came to be contracted, might be acknowledged the debt of every individual part of the whole Empire, Asia, as well as America, included.— Provided, that full security were held forth to them, that such free aids, together with the Sinking Fund (Great Britain contributing her superior share) should not be left as the privy purse of the minister, but be unalienably appropriated to the original intention of that fund, the discharge of the debt;—and that by an honest application of the *whole* fund, the taxes might in time be lessened, and the price of our manufactures consequently reduced, so that every contributory part might feel the returning benefit— always supposing the laws of trade duly observed and enforced.

"The time *was,* I am confident—and perhaps *is,* when these points might be obtained upon the easy, the constitutional, and, therefore, the indispensible terms of an exemption from parliamentary taxation, and an admission of the sacredness of their charters; instead of sacrificing their good humour, their affection, their effectual aids, and the act of NAVIGATIONitself, (which you are now in the direct road to do) for a commercial quit-rent,(a) or a barren metaphysical chimæra.—How long these ends may continue attainable, no man can tell.—But if no words are to be relied on except such as make against the Colonies— If nothing is acceptable, except what is attainable by force; it only remains to apply, what has been so often remarked of unhappy periods,—*Quos Deus vult, &c.*"

These are sentiments and proposals of the last importance; and I am very happy in being able to give them to the public from so respectable an authority, as that of the distinguished Peer I have mentioned; to whom, I know, this kingdom, as well as America, is much indebted for his zeal to promote those grand public points on which the preservation of Liberty among us depends; and for the firm opposition which, jointly with many others (Noblemen and Commoners of the first character and abilities,) he has made to the present measures.

Had such a plan as that now proposed been adopted a few months ago, I have little doubt but that a pacification would have taken place, on terms highly advantageous to this kingdom.—In particular. It is probable, that the Colonies would have consented to grant an annual supply, which, increased by a saving of the money now spent in maintaining troops among them, and by contributions which might have been gained from other parts of the Empire, would have formed a fund considerable enough, if unalienably applied(b), to redeem the public debt; in consequence of which, agreeably to Lord Shelburne's ideas, some of our worst taxes might be taken off, and the Colonies would receive our manufactures cheaper; our paper-currency might be restrained; our whole force would be free to meet at any time foreign danger; the influence of the Crown would be reduced; our Parliament would become more independent; and the kingdom might, perhaps, be restored to a situation of permanent safety and prosperity.

]

To conclude.—An important revolution in the affairs of this kingdom seems to be approaching. If ruin is not to be our lot, all that has been lately done must be undone, and new measures adopted. At that period, an opportunity (never perhaps to be recovered, if lost) will offer itself for serving essentially *this country*, as well as *America*; by putting the national debt into *a fixed* course of payment; by subjecting to new regulations, the administration of the finances; and establishing measures for exterminating corruption and restoring the constitution.—For my own part; if this is not to be the consequence of any future changes in the ministry, and the system of corruption, lately so much improved, is to go on; I think it totally indifferent to the kingdom who are *in,* or who are *out* of power.

APPENDIX.

Amount of
the NATIONAL DEBT, *and* APPROPRIATEDREVENUE, *at Midsummer* 1775.

	Principal.	Interest.
	£.	£.

*(a)*This deduction was not made in the former editions of this work. I should have thanked the writer who has pointed out this omission to me, had he done it in a handsomer manner. But nothing depends on this omission; nor does it affect the conclusion with a view to which I have chosen to state the national debt.

*(a)*Being charges of management at the Bank, South-Sea House and India Houses; Fees, Salaries and other Expences at the Exchequer; Interest of loans on the Sinking Fund; Annuities payable to the Dukes of Gloucester and Cumberland, and the Representatives of Arthur Onflow, Esq; Sheriffs of England; expence of coinage; first fruits of the clergy, &c.—These Articles were omitted in the former Editions, and served to balance the overcharges of interest on the *Bank* and *India* capitals. I have probably under-rated them; but it cannot be expected that I should be able to give their exact amount. I leave, therefore, this part of the appropriated revenue to be corrected by those who are better informed.

The amount of the capitals at the Bank, South Sea, and India Houses was (in January 1775) 125,056,454 l. See the particulars in an account by *R. Helm,* at the *Stock Exchange,* corrected for January 5th, 1775.

Deduct 2 millions Capital of India Annuit.; deduct	122.056,454	3.874,057

Amount of
the NATIONAL DEBT, *and* APPROPRIATEDREVENUE, *at*
Midsummer 1775.

	Principal.	Interest.
	£.	£.
also 424,500 l. Consol. Annuit. 246,300 l. Reduced; 161,650 l. Old S. S. Annuit. 124,200 l. New S. S. Annuit. and 43,350 l. Annuit. 1751, making in all a million of the 3 *per cents,* paid off in 1775; and the remainder will be		
Deduct farther, from the annual interest in Mr. *Helm*'s account, (besides the *Long Annuity,* and the interest of three millions at 3 *per cent.)* 383,814 l. being the amount of the excesses of the *Dividend,* (a) paid by the three companies above the interest they receive from government:		
Undivided Capital of the *Bank,* making up the whole to 11,6 6,800 l.	906,800	27,204
Annuities for 99, 96, and 89 years, from various dates in King William's and Queen Ann's time. Supposing 18 years to come of these Annuities, their value will be (reckoning interest at 3½ *per cent.)* 13⅓ years purchase, or nearly	1.801,179	136,453
Annuities for lives, with benefit of survivorship, in King William's time, supposed worth Four years purchase.—N. B. The benefit of survivorship is to be continued till the Annuitants are reduced to Seven	30,268	7,567
Annuities on lives, with benefit of Survivorship, granted Anno 1765—valued at 20 years purchase	10,800	540
Carried over	124.805,501	4.045,821
Brought over	124.805,501	4.045,821
Annuities for two or three lives granted in 1693. Also annuities on single lives 1745, 1746, 1757. The original amount of these annuities, taken all together, was 123,883 l. They are now reduced by deaths to about 80,000 l. I have valued them at 10 years purchase	800,000	80,000

Amount of
the NATIONAL DEBT, and APPROPRIATED REVENUE, at
Midsummer 1775.

	Principal.	Interest.
	£.	£.
Long annuity for 99 years 1761—The value of this annuity is in the *Alley* about 25½ years purchase; but the remaining term is really worth 27 years purchase	6.702,750	248,250
UNFUNDED DEBT, consisting of Exchequer Bills (1,250,000 l.) Navy debt (1,850,000 l.) and Civil List debt, supposed 500,000 l. The interest is reckoned at no more than 2½ *per cent.*	3.600,000	90,000
Total of the National debt in 1775	135.908,251	4.464,071
Add(a)		200,000
Civil List		800,000
Total of the appropriated Revenue		5.494,071

I have given the *Navy Debt* as it was about a year ago. It must be now greatly increased.—The *Civil List Debt* has been given by guess. It is generally reckoned not to be more than the sum I have specified; and it is also expected that the Civil List income will be raised to 900,000 l. or 1.000,0000 *per ann.*—In 1769 the sum of 513,511 l. was granted by parliament towards discharging the arrears and debts then due on the Civil List.

By an act of the first of George II, the income of the Civil List was to be made up to 800,000 l. whenever, in any year, the duties and revenues appropriated to it fell short of that sum. The clear produce of these duties for 33 years, or from Midsummer 1727, to Midsummer 1760, was, according to a particular account in my possession, 26.182,981 l. 17 s. 6 d. or 793,423 l. *per ann.* They fell short, therefore, taking one year with another, *more* than they exceeded.—In 1747, they had been deficient for seven years together; and the whole deficiency amounted to 456,733 l. 16 s.—which, in conformity to the act I have mentioned, was made good to his majesty out of the supplies for that year.—In 1729 also, 115,000 l. was granted out of the supplies for the like reason.—This is all the money, received by his late majesty from parliament, towards supporting his houshold and the dignity of his civil government; or 810,749 l. *per ann.*—I have thought proper to state this matter to particularly here; because accounts grossly wrong have been given of it.

The amount of the National Debt, it has appeared, was last year 136 millions—The great deficiencies of last year, added to the extraordinary expences of the present year, will increase this debt considerably.—Drawing out, embodying,] and maintaining the militia in the last war, cost the nation near half a million *per ann.*—We cannot reckon upon a less expence in doing this now. Add to it, pay for foreign troops, and all the extraordinary expences of our increased Navy and Army, transport service, recruiting service, ordnance, &c. and it will be evident that the whole expence of this unhappy year must be enormous.—But I expect that care will be taken to hide it, by funding as little as possible, and that for this reason it will not be known in its full magnitude, till it comes to appear another year under the articles of Navy debt, extraordinaries of the army, transport bills, ordnance debentures, &c. making up a vast unsunded debt which may bear down all public credit.

State of the SURPLUS *of the* REVENUE *for* 11 *years ended at*1775. UNAPPROPRIATED REVENUE.

£.

(a)The greatest part of this Revenue is borrowed of the Bank, and spent before it comes into the Exchequer. And therefore, is a debt constantly due to the Bank, for which interest is paid.—One of my answerers has denied this

State of the SURPLUS of the REVENUE for 11 years ended at 1775. UNAPPROPRIATED REVENUE.

£.

assertion; but at the same time has confirmed it, by saying that only 2.250,000 l. was borrowed in 1775 on the unappropriated Revenue.—The same writer has asserted, that there are THREE MILLIONS of *India* Annuities created by the company itself, and that this makes TWO MILLIONS difference in the amount of the national debt.—The truth is, that in consequence of taking Mr. *Helm*'s paper (a paper perfectly adapted to the purpose for which it is intended) without examining it; I had made the capital of the perpetual Annuities to be 124.056,454 l.; whereas, if two millions *India*Annuities are rejected, and 906,800 l. undivided capital of the *Bank*admitted, it comes out to be 122.963,254 l. See p. 41.—The writer who has given to the public this information, received it, I understand, from the great ministe who directs our Finances, to whose Authority on this subject I am very ready to submit. Pity it is, that he did not choose to communicate it by a person possess'd of more of his own ability and candour.

	£.
NETT PRODUCE of the Sinking Fund for the last five years, including casual surplusses, reckoning to *Christmas* in every year; being the annual medium, after deducing from it about 45,000 l. always carried to it from the supplies, in order to replace so much taken from it every year to make good a deficiency in a Fund established in 1758	2.610,759
Nett annual produce of Land Tax at 3 s. militia deducted; and of the Malt Tax	1.800,000
(N. B. These two taxes in 1773, brought in only 1.665,475 l.	
There are some casual Receipts, not included in the Sinking Fund, such as duties on Gum Senega, American Revenue, &c. But they are so uncertain and inconsiderable, that it is scarcely proper to give them as a part of the permanent Revenue. Add however on this account	50,000
	£.
Total of unappropriated (*a*) Revenue	4.460,759

Produce of the SINKING FUND, reckoned to Christmas in every Year.

	£.
1770	2.486,836
1771	2.553,505

80

State of the SURPLUS *of the* REVENUE *for* 11 *years ended at* 1775. UNAPPROPRIATED REVENUE.

	£.
1772	2.603,831
1773	2.823,150
1774	2.731,476

In 1775 the sinking Fund was taken for 2.900,000 l. including an extraordinary charge of 100,000 l. on the *Aggregate* Fund. If it has not produced so much,] the deficiency is a debt contracted last year, which must be added to other debts (referred to in Page 43) arising from deficiencies in the provision made for the expences of last year. This provision amounted to 3.703,476 l.; but it has fallen short above a million and a half.(*n*)

ANNUAL EXPENDITURE.

	£.
Peace Establishment, for the Navy and Army, including all miscellaneous and incidental expences	3.700,000
Annual Increase of the Navy and Civil List Debts	350,000
Interest at 2 1/2 of 3,600,000 l. unfunded debt, which must be paid out of the unappropriated Revenue	90,000
Total	4.140,000
ANNUAL SURPLUS of the Revenue	320,759
Annual income	£. 4.460,759

The estimate for the peace establishment, including miscellaneous expences, amounted, I have said, in 1775 to 3.703,476 l.—In 1774 it amounted to 3.804,452 l. exclusive of 250,000 l. raised by Exchequer Bills, towards defraying the expence of calling in the gold coin. And the medium for eleven years, from 1765, has been nearly 3.700,000 l.—

According to the accounts which I have collected, the expence of the peace establishment (including miscellaneous expences) was in 1765, 1766, and 1767, 3.540,000 l. *per ann.*—In 1768, 1769, and 1770, it was 3.354,000 l. *per ann.*—In 1771, 1772, 1773, 1774, and 1775, the average has been nearly four millions *per ann.* exclusive of the expence of calling in the coin.

The parliament votes for the sea service 4 l. *per* month *per*man, including wages, wear and tear, victuals and ordnance. This allowance is insufficient, and falls short every year more or less, in proportion to the number of men voted. From hence, in a great measure, arises that annual increase of the navy debt, mentioned in the second article of the *National Expenditure.* This increase in 1772 and 1773 was 669,996 l. or 335,000 l. *per ann.* The number of men voted in those two years, was 20,000. I have supposed them reduced to 16,000, and the annual increase of the Navy Debt to be only 250,000 l.— Add 100,000 l. for the annual increase of the Civil List Debt (see p. 42.) and the total will be 350,000 l.

There is another method of proving that the permanent surplus of the revenue cannot exceed the sum now stated.

I have learnt from the highest authority, that the national debt, about a year ago, had been diminished near 9 millions and a half,(*b*) since the peace in 1763; including a million of the 3 *per cents* discharged last year.—The money employed in making this reduction, must have been derived from the surplus of the *ordinary* and stated revenue, added to the *extraordinary* receipts. These *extraordinary* receipts have consisted of the following articles.—1. The Land Tax at 4 s. in the pound in 1764, 1765, 1766, and 1771; or 1 s. in the pound *extraordinary* for four years, making 1.750,000 l.—2. The profits of Ten Lotteries, making (at

150,000 l. each Lottery) 1.500,000 l.—3. A contribution of 400,000 l. *per ann.* from the *India* company for five years, making 2.000,000 l.—4. 110,000 l.] Paid by the Bank in 1764 for the privilege of exclusive banking. Also the money Paid by *France* for maintaining their prisoners; and the money arising from the sale of *French* prizes, taken before the declaration of war; from savings on particular grants at the end of the war, &c. &c.—which(*a*) I will take at no more than 300,000 l. Add 3.600,000 l. arising from a surplus of 300,000 l. for twelve years; and the total will be 9.260,000 l. which is a sum more than sufficient to discharge 9 millions and a half of the public debt.

Sketch of an Account of the Money drawn from the Public by the Taxes.

£.

(*b*)The annual medium of the payments into the Exchequer from the Customs in England, for the last five years, has been 2.521,769 l.—In 1774 this payment was 2.547,717 l. In 1775, it was 2.476,302 l.—The produce of the Customs, therefore, has been given rather too high.
The produce of the Excises in England has been higher in 1772 and 1775 than in any other two years; but the average of any three successive years, or of all the five years since 1770, will not differ much from the sum I have given.—In 1754, or the year before the last war, the Customs produced only 1.558,254 l.—The Excises produced 2.819,702 l.—And the whole revenue, exclusive of the Malt-tax and Land-tax at 2 s. was 5.097,617 l.

(*c*)These branches of the revenue produced in 1754 210,243 l. I do not know how much they have produced lately; but I believe I have estimated them at the highest.—In 1754 the Revenue of the Post-Office was 100,710 l. It brought in last year 125,000 l.

	£.
Customs in England, being the medium of the payments into the Exchequer, for 3 years ending in 1773(*b*)	2.528,275
Amount of the Excises in England, including the malt tax, being the medium of 3 years ending in 1773	4.649,892
Land Tax at 3 s.	1.300,000
Land Tax at 1 s. in the pound	450,000
Salt Duties, being the medium of the years 1765 and 1766	218,739

Sketch of an Account of the Money drawn from the Public by the Taxes.

	£.
Duties on Stamps, Cards, Dice, Advertisements, Bonds, Leases, Indentures, News-papers, Almanacks, &c.	280,788
Duties on houses and windows, being the medium of 3 years ending in 1771	385,369
Post-Office, Seizures, Wine Licences, Hackney Coaches,(c)Tenths of the Clergy, &c.	250,000
Excises in Scotland, being the medium of 3 years ending in 1773	95,229
Customs in Scotland, being the medium of 3 years ending in 1773	68,369
Annual profit from Lotteries	150,000
Inland taxes in Scotland, deduction of 6 d. in the pound on all Pensions, Salaries, &c. casual revenues, such as the duties on Gum-Senega, American revenue, &c.	150,000
Expence of collecting the Excises in England, being the average of the years 1767 and 1768, when their produce was 4.531,075 l. *per ann.* 6 *per cent.* of the gross produce	297,887
Expence of collecting the Excises in Scotland, being the medium of the years 1772 and 1773, and the difference between the gross and nett produce—31 *per cent.* of the gross produce	43,254
Expence of collecting the Customs in England, being the average of 1771 and 1772; bounties included—15 *per cent.* of the gross produce, exclusive of drawbacks and over-entries	468,703
N. B. The bounties for 1771 were 202,840 l. for 1772, 172,468 l.	
The charges of management for 1771, were 276,434 l.	
For 1772, 285,764 l. or 10 *per cent.* nearly.	
Interest of loans on the land tax at 4 l. expences of collection, militia, &c.	250,000
Perquisites, &c. to Custom-house officers, &c. supposed	250,000
Expence of collecting the Salt Duties in England, 10½ *per cent.*	27,000

Sketch of an Account of the Money drawn from the Public by the Taxes.

	£.
Bounties on fish exported	18,000
EXPENCE of collecting the duties on Stamps, Cards, Advertisements, &c. 5¼ *per cent.*	18,000
Total £.	11.900,505

It must be seen, that this account is imperfect. It is, however, sufficient to prove, that the whole money raised DIRECTLY by the taxes, cannot be much less than TWELVE MILLIONS. But as the increased price of one commodity has a tendency to raise the price of other commodities; and as also dealers generally add more than the value of a tax to the price of a commodity, besides charging interest for the money they advance on the taxes; for these reasons, it seems certain, that the taxes have an INDIRECT effect of great consequence; and that a larger sum is drawn by them from the public, than their *gross* produce.—It is farther to be considered, that many of the persons who are now supported by collecting the taxes, would have supported themselves by commerce or agriculture; and therefore, instead of taking away from the public stock, would have been employed in increasing it.—Some have reckoned, that on all these accounts the expence of the taxes is *doubled;* but this must be extravagant. Let us suppose a *fourth* only added; and it will follow, that the money drawn from the public by the taxes (exclusive of tythes, county-rates, and the taxes which maintain the poor) is near 15 millions *per ann.;* a sum equal to the whole specie of the kingdom; which, therefore, had we no paper currency, would be totally inadequate to the wants of the kingdom.

Without all doubt such a state of things, in a great commercial nation, is most dangerous, and frightful; but it admits of no remedy, while the public debt continues what it is.—With a view, therefore, to the quick reduction of this debt, I will throw away, after all I have said on this subject on former occasions, the following proposals.—It has appeared, that, supposing the taxes not to become less productive, and the current national expence to continue the same that it had been for ten years before 1775, a surplus may be expected in the revenue of about 300,000 l. *per ann.*—With a surplus so trifling, nothing can be done; but it might be increased, first of all; By keeping the LAND TAX for the future at 4 s. in the pound.—As rents have been almost doubled, this will not be much more to the present proprietors of land, than 2 s. in the pound was formerly. 'Tis, therefore, equitable; and it will add to the national income near 450,000 l.

Secondly, All the money now spent in maintaining troops in America might be saved.—The Colonies are able to defend themselves. They wish to be allowed to do it. Should they ever want the aid of our troops, they will certainly pay us for them. Indeed I am of opinion, they will never be willing to make peace with us, without stipulating that we shall withdraw our troops from them. Were there any external power that claimed and exercised a right of stationing troops in this country, without our consent, we should certainly think ourselves entirely undone.—I will estimate this saving at no more than 200,000 l. *per ann.*

Thirdly, I do not see why the peace establishment might not be reduced to what it was, at an average, in 1768, 1769 and 1770. This would produce a saving of 350,000 *l. per ann.*— I might here propose reducing the peace establishment for the *Navy* to what it always was before the last war, or from 16,000 to 10,000 men. But it would be infinitely better to reduce the ARMY; and this might produce a farther saving of great consequence.—But waving this, I shall only mention,

]

Fourthly, That contributions might be obtained from *North-America* and other parts of the British Empire, on the principles stated from the EARL of SHELBURNE's authority, in page 39.—I will estimate these at no more than 400,000 l. *per ann.*—(d) Add the *Surplus* now in our possession; and the total will be 1.700,000.— In the *Introduction* to the third edition of the Treatise on *Reversionary Payments,* I have explained a method of paying off, with a sinking Fund of a million *per ann.*(b), a hundred millions of the national debt in forty years. What then might not be done with such a Fund as this?

In five years 18.986,300 l. will fall from an interest of 4 *per cent.* to 3 *per cent.*—Also, 4.500,000 l. 31/7 *per cent.* 1758, will fall, in six years, to an interest of 3 *per cent.*—The long Annuities granted in King WILLIAM's time, will, in 20 years become extinct; as will also the greatest part of the Life Annuities specified in page 41.—All these savings will not amount to much less than 400,000 l. *per ann.* And were they to be added to the fund as they fall in, its operations would be so much accelerated, that in a few years we should see this country above all its difficulties.—Still more might be done by striking off unnecessary places and pensions; by giving up all the means of corruption; by reducing the pay of the great officers of state; and simplifying the taxes.—A minister who appeared determined to carry into execution such a system, would soon gain the confidence of the public; endear himself to all honest men; and in time come to be blessed as the Saviour of his country.—But what am I doing?—We have no such happy period before us.—Our ministers are active in pursuing measures which must increase our burthens. A horrid civil war is begun; and it may soon leave us nothing to be anxious about.

POSTSCRIPT.

ACCOUNT of Public debts discharged, Money borrowed, and Annual Interest saved, from 1763 to 1775.

Debts paid off since 1763.				Annuity decreased.	
	£.			£.	*s.*
1765	870,888	funded, bearing interest at	*4 per cent.*	34,835	10
	1.500,006	unfunded,	*4 per cent.*	60,000	00
1766	0.870,888	funded,	*4 per cent.*	34,835	10
	1.200,000	unfunded,	4	48,000	00
1767	2.616,777	funded,	4	104,671	0
1768	2.625,000	funded,	4	105,000	0
1771	1.500,000	funded,	*3½ per cent.*	52,500	0
1772	1.500,000	funded,	*3 per cent.*	45,000	0
1773	800,000	unfunded,	3	24,000	0
1774	1.000,000	funded,	3	30,000	0
1775	1.000,000	funded,	3	30,000	0
	Total 15.483,553			Total — 568,842	0

]

In 1764, there was paid off 650,000 *l.* navy-debt; but this I have not charged, because scarcely equal to that annual increase of the navy-debt for 1764, 1765, and 1766, which forms a part of the ordinary peace establishment. The same is true of 300,000 *l.* navy-debt, paid in 1767; of 400,000 *l.*paid in 1769; of 100,200 *l.* paid in 1770; 200,000 *l.* in 1771; 215,883 *l.* in 1772; and 200,000 *l.* in 1774.

Account of money borrowed since 1763.

	£.	Annual interest increased.
Borrowed and funded, at 3 *per cent.* in 1765	1.500,000	45,000
in 1766	1.500,000	45,000
in 1767	1.500,000	45,000
in 1768	1.900,000	57,000
Unfunded in 1774	250,000	7,500
	Total — 6.650,000	199,500

From 15.483,553 *l.* the total of debts discharged, subtract 6.650,000 *l.* the total of debts contracted; and the remainder, or 8.833,553 *l.* will be the diminution of the public debts since 1763. Also, from 568,842 *l.* the total of the decrease of the annual interest, subtract 199,500 *l.* (the total of its increase), and the remainder, or 369,342 *l.* will be the interest or annuity saved since 1763—To this must be added 12,537 *l. per ann.* saved by changing a capital of 1.253,700 *l.*(part of 20.240,000 *l.*) from an interest of 4 to 3 *per cent.*pursuant to an act of the 10th of George III.; also the lifeannuities that have fallen in; which will make a saving in the whole of near 400,000 *l. per annum:* And it is to this saving, together with the increase of luxury, that the increase of the *Sinking Fund* for the last ten years has been owing.

To the debts discharged the following additions must be made.

In 1764 there was paid towards discharging the extraordinary expences of the army, 987,434 *l.:* In 1765, these expences amounted to 404,496 *l.:* In 1766, to 404,310 *l.*—Total 1.796,240 *l.*—This sum is at least a million higher than the extraordinary expences of the army for three years in a time of peace. This excess being derived from the preceding war, must be reckoned a debt left by the war. And the same is true of 1.106,000 *l.* applied, in 1764, 1765, and 1766, towards satisfying *German* demands.— There are likewise some smaller sums of the same kind; such as subsidies to *Hesse-Cassel, Brunswick,* &c. And they may be taken at 200,000 *l.*—The total of all these Sums is 2.306,240 *l.;* which, added to 8.833,553 *l.* makes the whole diminution of the public debt since 1763, to be 11.139,793 *l.*—Towards discharging this debt, the nation, besides the surplus of its ordinary revenue, has received, at different times between the years 1763 and 1768, from savings on high grants during the war, from the produce of *French* prizes, from the Bank for the renewal of their charter, from the sale of lands in the ceded islands, and composition for maintaining *French*prisoners(a), 2.630,000 *l.* Also, from the profits of ten(b)lotteries (at 150,000 *l.* each lottery) 1.500,000 *l.;* from the *East-India* Company (400,000 *l. per ann.* for five years) 2.000,000 *l.;* from 1*s.* extraordinary land-tax for 4 years, 1.750,000 *l.;* from debts discharged at a discount, 400,000 *l.;*(c): In all 8.280,000 *l.*—There remains to make up 11.139,793 *l.* (the whole debt discharged) 2.859,793 *l.;* and this, therefore, is the amount of the whole surplus of the ordinary revenue for 12 years; or 238,000 *l. per annum.*

Soon after the peace in 1763, an unfunded debt, amounting to 6.983,553 *l*. was funded on the *Sinking Fund,* and on new duties on wine and cyder at 4 *per cent.* There has been since borrowed and funded on coals exported, window-lights, &c. 6.400,000 *l*. The funded debt, therefore, has increased since the war 13.383,553 *l*. It has decreased (as appears from page 47) 11.983,553 *l.;* and, consequently, these has been on the whole an addition to it of 1.400,000 *l*.—During seven years, from 1767 to 1774, 1.415,883 *l*. navy-debt was paid off. See above. But, as this is a debt arising from constant deficiencies in the peace estimates for the navy, it is a part of the current peace expences. —In 1768 this debt was(*a*)1.226,915 *l*.—In 1774 it was 1.850,000 *l.;* and consequently, though 1.415,883 *l*. was paid off an addition was made to it, seven years, of 623,085 *l*. It encreased, therefore, according to this account, at the rate of 291,000 *l. per ann.*

Upon the whole, there is reason to believe, that the annual increase of the navy-debt might have been more truly stated in page 44. at 300,000 *l. per ann.* and this would have reduced the annual surplus of the revenue to 270.759 *l. per annum.*

FINIS.

(a)

In *Great Britain,* consisting of near six *millions* of inhabitants, 5723 persons, most of them the lowest of the people, elect one half of the *House of Commens;* and 364 votes chuse a ninth part. This may be seen distinctly made out in the *Political Disquisitions,* Vol. I. Book 2. C. 4. a work full of important and useful instruction.

(a)

See among others Mr. Locke on Government, and Dr. Priestley's Essay on the first Principles of Government.

(b)

See Dr. Priestley on Government, page 68, 69, &c.

(a)

The independency of the Judges we esteem in this country one of our greatest privileges.—Before the revolution they generally, I believe, held their places *during pleasure.* King William gave them their places *during good behaviour.* At the accession of the present Royal Family their places were given them *during good behaviour,* in consequence of the Act of Settlement, 12 and 13 W. III. C. 2. But an opinion having been entertained by some, that though their commissions were made under the Act of Settlement to continue, during good behaviour, yet that they determined on the demise of the Crown; it was enacted by a statute made in the first year of his present Majesty, Chap. 23. "That the commissions of Judges for the time being shall be, continue, and remain in full force, during their good behaviour, notwithstanding the demise of his Majesty, or of any of his Heirs and Successors;" with a proviso, "that it may be lawful for his Majesty, his Heirs and Successors, to remove any Judge upon the address of both Houses of Parliament." And by the same Statute their salaries are secured to them during the continuance of their commissions: His Majesty, according to the preamble of the Statute, having been pleased to declare from the Throne to both Houses of Parliament, "That he looked upon the independency and uprightness of Judges as essential to the impartial administration of Justice, at one of the best securities to the Rights and Liberties of his loving subjects, and as most conducive to the honour of his Crown."

A worthy friend and able Lawyer has supplied me with this note. It affords, when contrasted with that *dependence* of the Judges which has been thought reasonable in *America,* a sad specimen of the different manner in which a kingdom may think proper to govern itself, and the provinces subject to it.

(a)

Montesquieu's Spirit of Laws, Vol. I. Book 11. C. xix.

(a)

This is particularly true of the *bounties* granted on some American commodities (as pitch, tar, indigo, &c.) when imported into *Britain;* for it is well known, that the end of granting them was, to get those commodities cheaper from the Colonies, and in return for our manufactures, which we used to get from *Russia* and other foreign countries. And this is expressed in the preambles of the laws which grant these bounties. See the Appeal to the Justice, &c. page 21, third edition. It is, therefore, strange that Doctor TUCKER and others, should have insisted so much upon these bounties as favours and indulgences to the Colonies.—But it is still more strange, that the time representation should have been made of the compensations granted them for doing more during the last war in assisting us than could have been reasonably expected; and also of the sums we have spent in maintaining troops among them *without* their consent; and in opposition to their wishes.—See a pamphlet, intitled "The rights of Great Britain asserted against the claims of America."

(a)

It gives me pleasure to find, that the author of the *Remarks on the Principal Acts of the* 13*th Parliament of Great Britain,* &c. acknowledges this difference.—It has, however, been at the same time mortifying to me to find so able a writer adopting such principles of government, as are contained in this work. According to him, a people have no property or rights, except such as their *Civil Governers* are pleased not to take from them. Taxes, therefore, he asserts, are in no tense the *gift,* much less the *free gifts* of the people. See p. 58. and 191.

(*a*)

See Observations on Reversionary Payments, page 207, &c.

(*a*)

See page 12.

(*a*)

The author of *Taxation no Tyranny* will undoubtedly assert this without hesitation; for in page 69 he compares our present sitution with respect to the Colonies to that of the antient *Scythians,* who, upon returning from a war *found themselves shut out of their own* HOUSES *by their*SLAVES.

(*b*)

See particularly, a Speech intended to have been spoken on the bill for altering the Charter of the Colony of Massachuset's Bay; the *Considerations on the Measures carrying on with respect to the British Colonies;* the *Two Appeals to the Justice and Interests of the People;* and the *further Examination* (just published) *of our present*

American Measures, by the Author of the Considerations, &c.

(*a*)

I have heard it said by a person in one of the first departments of the state, that the present contest is for DOMINION on the side of the Colonies, as well as on ours: And so it is, indeed; but with this essential difference. *We* are struggling for dominion over OTHERS. *They* are struggling for SELF-dominion: The noblest of all blessings.

(*a*)

This has been our policy with respect to the people of *Ireland;* and the consequence is, that we now their parliament as obedient as we can wish.

(a)

Excepting the *Negroes* in the Southern Colonies, who probably will now either soon become extinct, or have their condition changed into that of *Freemen.*—It is not the fault of the Colonies that they have among them so many of these unhappy people. They have made laws to prohibit the importation of them; but these laws have always had a negative put upon them here, because of their tendency to hurt our Negro trade.

(b)

In the County of Suffolk, where Boston is, there has not been, I am informed, more than one execution these 18 years.

(c)

Mr. Burke (in his excellent and admirable Speech on moving his resolutions for conciliation with the Colonies, P. 9, &c.) has shewn, that our trade to the Colonies, including that to *Africa* and the *West-Indies,* was in 1773 nearly equal to the trade which we carried on with the whole world at the beginning of this Century.

(a)

See Dr. Davenant's works, collected and revised by Sir Charles Whitworth, Vol. I. Page 363, &c. 443, &c.

(b)

See Considerations on Money, Bullion, &c. Page 2 and 11.

(c)

Or nearly the same that it was in *Cromwell*'s time. See Dr. Davenant's works, Vol. I. Page 365.

(a)

See Sir James Steuart's Enquiry into the Principles of political Occonomy, Vol. II. Book 4. Chap. 32.

(b)

Their debts consist chiefly of money raised by annuities on lives, short annuities, anticipations of taxes for short terms, &c. During the whole last war they added to their *perpetual* annuities only 12 millions sterling, according to Sir James Steuart's account; whereas we added to these annuities near 60 millions. In consequence therefore of the nature of their debts, as well as of the management they are now using for hastening the reduction of them, they must in a few years, if peace continues, be freed from most of their incumbrances; while we probably (if no event comes soon that will unburthen us at once, shall continue with them all upon us.

(a)

Mr. *Lowndes* in the dispute between him and Mr. *Locke,* contended for a reduction of the standard of silver. One of his reasons was, that it would render the silver-coin more commensurate to the wants of the nation; and CHECK HAZARDOUS PAPER-CREDIT.—Mr. CONDUIT, Sir ISAAC NEWTON's successor in the mint, has proposed, in direct contradiction to the laws now in being, that all the bullion imported into the kingdom should be carried into the mint to be coined; and only coin allowed to be exported. "The height, he says, of Paper-credit is the strongest argument for trying this and *every other* method that is likely to increase the coinage.. For whilst Paper-credit does in a great measure the business of money at home, Merchants and Bankers are not under a necessity, as they were formerly, of coining a quantity of specie for their home trade; and as Paper-credit brings money to the Merchants to be exported, the money may go away insensibly, and NOT BE MISSED TILL IT BE TOO LATE: And where Paper-credit is large and increasing, if the money be exported and the coinage decrease, THAT CREDIT MAY SINK AT ONCE; for want of a proportionable quantity of *Specie,* which alone can support it in a time of distress."—See Mr. *Conduit*'s Observations on the state of our Gold and Silver Coins in 1730, Page 36 to 46.

(a)

According to the accounts of the exports to, and imports from the North-American Colonies, laid before Parliament; the balance in our favour appears to have been, for 11 years before 1774, near a *million and a half* annually.

(a)

See the substance of the evidence on the petition presented by the *West-India* Planters and Merchants to the House of Commons, as it was introduced at the BAR, and summed up by Mr. GLOVER.

(b)

The annual average of the payments into the Exchequer, on account of the duties on tobacco, was for five years, from 1770 to 1774, 219,117 l. exclusive of the payments from *Scotland.*—Near one half of the *tobacco* trade is carried on from *Scotland;* and above *four fifths* of the tobacco imported is afterwards exported to *France, Germany* and other countries. From *France* alone it brings annually into the Kingdom, I am informed, about 150,000 l. in money.

In 1775, being, alas! the *parting* year, the duties on tobacco in ENGLAND brought into the *Exchequer* no less a sum than 298,202 l.

(c)

See the Append x.

(a)

A quarter of the inhabitants of every country are fighting men.—If, therefore, the Colonies consist only of two millions of inhabitants, the number of fighting men in them will be half a million.

(b)

See the Appendix to Dr. Zubly's Sermon, preached at the opening of the Provincial Congress of *Georgia.*

(c)

NEW YORK has been long deserted by the greatest part of the inhabitants; and they are determined to burn it themselves, rather than suffer us to burn it.

(a)

"I have no other notion of slavery, but being bound by a law to which I do not consent." See the case of *Ireland's* being bound by acts of Parliament in *England,* stated by William Molyneux, Esq; Dublin.—In arguing against the authority of Communities, and all people not incorporated, over one another; I have confined my views to taxation and internal legislation. Mr. Molyneux carried his views much farther; and denied the right of *England* to make any laws even to regulate the trade of *Ireland.* He was the intimate friend of Mr. Locke; and writ his book in 1698, soon after the publication of Mr. Locke's Treatise on Government.

What I have said, in Part 1st. Sect. 3d. of subjecting a number of states to a general council representing them all, I suppose every one must consider as entirely theoretical; and not a proposal of any thing I wish, may take place under the British Empire.

(b)

Some persons, convinced of the *folly* as well as *barbarity* of attempting to keep the Colonies by slaughtering them, have very humanely proposed giving them up. But the highest authority has informed us, with great reason, "That they are too important to be given up."—Dr. TUCKER has insisted on the depopulation, produced by migrations from this country to the Colonies, as a reason for this measure. But, unless the kingdom is made a prison to its inhabitants, these migrations cannot be prevented; nor do I think that they have any great tendency to produce depopulation. When a number of people quit a country, there is more employment and greater plenty of the means of subsistence lest for those who remain; and the vacancy is soon filled up. The grand causes of depopulation are, not migrations, or even famines and plagues, or any other *temporary* evils; but the permanent and slowly-working evils of debauchery, luxury, high taxes, and oppression.

(a)

See the Resolutions on the *Nova-Scotia* petition reported to the House of Commons, November 29, 1775, by Lord North, Lord George Germaine, &c. and a bill ordered to be brought in upon the said Resolutions.—There is indeed, as Lord Shelburne has hinted, something very astonishing in these Resolutions. They offer a relaxation of the authority of this country, in points to which the Colonies have always consented, and by which we are great gainers; at the same time, that, with a rigour which hazards the Empire, we are maintaining its authority in points to which they will never consent; and by which nothing can be gained.

(b)

See the Appendix.

(a)

The expences of the army not provided for in 1775 have amounted to 845,000 l. spent chiefly at *Boston.*—The Navy debt increased, during the course of the same year, from 1.850,000 l. to 2.498,579 l.

(b)

This was Lord *North*'s account at opening the budget in 1775. The particulars, as I have been able to collect them, I have stated in the Postscript.

(a)

My reason for this will be seen in the Postscript, page 48.

(a)

We drew, some years ago, this contribution from ASIAonly: and it cannot be unreasonable to expect, that the greatest part of it may be again drawn from thence after the expiration, in 1780, of the charter of the EAST-INDIA company. At that period also, it is much to be wished that some effectual measures may be established for making amends to the inhabitants of BENGAL for the shocking injuries they have suffered; and for skreening them from all farther injuries; and, likewise, for withdrawing from the crown that Patronage of the East India Company, which it has lately acquired, and which has given one of the deepest wounds to the constitution.

(b)

At the time of writing the introduction here referred to, above three years ago, I *thought,* or rather *hoped,* that the surplus of the revenue might be taken at 900,000 l. *per ann.* But it must be considered, that the nation was then in possession of a contribution of 400,000 l. *per ann.* from the India Company, which has been since lost—See the Additional Preface to the 2d Edition *of the Appeal to the Public on the Subject of the National Debt.*

(*a*)

See the particulars in a pamphlet entitled, *The present State of the nation,* published in 1768. Page 56.

(*b*)

Four of these lotteries have been annexed to annuities; but it is a great mistake to think that they have not been equally profitable with the other lotteries. For instance: In 1767 a million and a half was borrowed on annuities, at 3 *per cent.* with a lottery of 60,000 tickets annexed.. In the same year 2.616,777 *l.* was paid off; but had it not been for the lottery, only 1.350,000 *l.* could have been raised on the annuities, and 10,000 *l.* left must have been paid off.

(*c*)

The discounts only on a million and a half paid off in 1772, and 2 millions paid off in 1774 and 1775, amounted nearly to this sum.

(*d*)

See *The present State of the Nation,* page 51.

Made in the USA
Middletown, DE
03 November 2023

41873773R10061